South Africa

South Africa

BY ETTAGALE BLAUER AND JASON LAURÉ

Enchantment of the World™
Second Series

Children's Press®

An Imprint of Scholastic Inc.

NEW YORK   TORONTO   LONDON   AUCKLAND   SYDNEY
MEXICO CITY   NEW DELHI   HONG KONG
DANBURY, CONNECTICUT

Frontispiece: Girl in Limpopo Province

Consultant: Robert R. Edgar, Professor, Howard University, Department of African Studies, Washington, DC

Please note: All statistics are as up-to-date as possible at the time of publication.

Book production by The Design Lab

Cataloging-in-Publication data is available from the Library of Congress.
ISBN 978-0-531-25603-9

1 2 3 4 5 6 7 8 9 10 R 22 21 20 19 18 17 16 15 14 13

South Africa

Contents

Cover photo:
Woman painted with
South African flag

Namaqualand

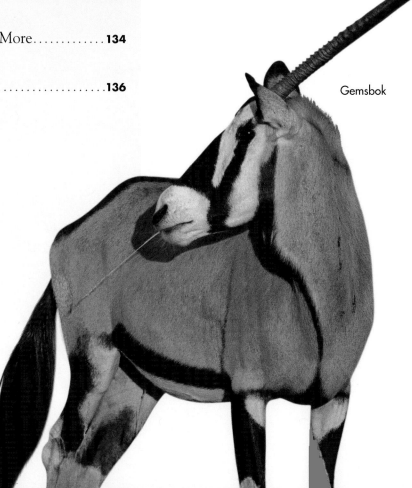

Gemsbok

Coming
of Age

IN THE WORLD OF NATIONS, THE REPUBLIC OF SOUTH Africa is still young. In 1994, when all adults in the nation were allowed to vote for the first time, they elected Nelson Mandela, a black African, as president. Until that time, only white people had been permitted to vote for president and for members of Parliament. The majority of people in South Africa, who were black or mixed race, were not allowed to vote.

Just four years earlier, Nelson Mandela had been in prison, serving a life sentence. He had already been in jail for twenty-seven years. His crime was working to change the political and social system called apartheid. The word means "separateness" in the Afrikaans language, one of the languages spoken in South Africa. Apartheid was designed to separate people into groups according to the color of their skin, their culture, and their ethnic differences.

Opposite: **A group of friends pose in Durban, one of South Africa's largest and most diverse cities.**

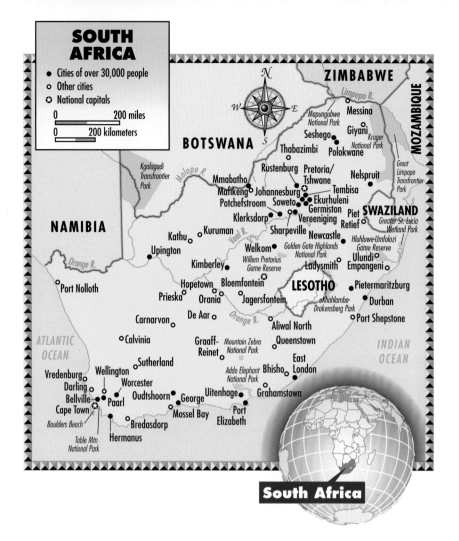

SOUTH AFRICA

- Cities of over 30,000 people
- Other cities
- National capitals

0 — 200 miles
0 — 200 kilometers

ZIMBABWE

MOZAMBIQUE

Limpopo R.

Mapungubwe National Park

Messina

Giyani

Kruger National Park

Seshego

Thabazimbi

Polokwane

Nelspruit

Great Limpopo Transfrontier Park

BOTSWANA

Kgalagadi Transfrontier Park

Molopo R.

Rustenburg

Pretoria/Tshwane

Mmabatho

Mafikeng

Johannesburg

Tembisa

Potchefstroom

Soweto

Ekurhuleni

Germiston

Vereeniging

Piet Retief

SWAZILAND

Klerksdorp

Sharpeville

Newcastle

Greater St. Lucia Wetland Park

NAMIBIA

Kathu

Kuruman

Vaal R.

Hluhluwe-Umfolozi Game Reserve

Upington

Welkom

Golden Gate Highlands National Park

Ladysmith

Ulundi

Empangeni

Orange R.

Kimberley

Willem Pretorius Game Reserve

Hopetown

Bloemfontein

LESOTHO

Pietermaritzburg

Port Nolloth

Prieska

Orania

Jagersfontein

uKhahlamba-Drakensberg Park

Durban

Carnarvon

De Aar

Orange R.

Aliwal North

Port Shepstone

ATLANTIC OCEAN

Calvinia

Graaff-Reinet

Mountain Zebra National Park

Queenstown

East London

INDIAN OCEAN

Sutherland

Bhisho

Vredenburg

Wellington

Worcester

Addo Elephant National Park

Grahamstown

Darling

Bellville

Paarl

Oudtshoorn

George

Uitenhage

Cape Town

Mossel Bay

Port Elizabeth

Boulders Beach

Bredasdorp

Table Mtn National Park

Hermanus

South Africa

Life Under Apartheid

For almost five decades, South Africa's all-white government had ruled under apartheid. It had insisted that each black ethnic group have separate "homelands." Black South Africans were assigned to these homelands, and the government claimed they were citizens of these homelands rather than of South Africa. The government created separate school systems for different racial groups. But these schools were not equal in any sense. The best of everything was kept for white South Africans, who made up just one-seventh of the population. The homelands for the black majority population accounted for just 13 percent of the nation's land. The white population kept the other 87 percent of the land.

Year after year, the all-white government passed more laws—hundreds and hundreds of them—intended to deny most of the population the right to lead a decent way of life. As a result, the government didn't spend much on the basic structures that a modern society needs. It didn't install electrical lines or clean water supplies to most of the areas where

Under apartheid, schools for black South Africans were crowded and had few supplies.

people of color lived. It didn't build roads into those areas. Whatever it did build was designed to move workers to areas where they were needed. Once the workday was over, black South Africans were supposed to go home. It was illegal for a black worker to be in a "white" city overnight after his or her job was done for the day. For some workers, that meant leaving home at 3:00 a.m., traveling by bus for hours to get to work, and then spending hours getting back home again at the end of the day. They had time only to sleep a few hours before starting the routine again the next day.

Police officers chase a man taking part in a protest in Cape Town in 1976.

The apartheid system was expensive to maintain. And money that was needed to invest in new schools, hospitals, and roads dried up as companies and governments around the world began boycotts against South Africa. They refused to do business with South Africa because it had such an unjust system of government. To pressure the South African government to end apartheid, countries throughout the world banned South Africans from competing in international events such as the Olympics and the World Cup soccer tournament. Many countries also barred South Africans from crossing their borders. Eventually, because of the protests both inside South Africa and in other countries, the white government agreed to end apartheid and allow the people to choose their own rulers.

Black South Africans march through the streets of Cape Town in 1960 to demand the release of antiapartheid leaders. People both inside and outside the country pressured South Africa to end its racist policies.

From time to time, a single event marks a turning point in the history of a nation. South Africa has had several of these, beginning in 1990 with the release of Nelson Mandela from prison. His election as president four years later was another.

The new South African government had to govern the nation while also struggling to undo the harm created by apartheid. This has been a long, hard process, and the cost of the old system is still being paid. Millions of people live

Nelson Mandela walks out of a prison in Paarl, in southwestern South Africa, on February 11, 1990. He had been in jail for twenty-seven years.

Nelson Mandela

Nelson Mandela stood at the center of South Africa's transition to democracy. His strength of character enabled him to survive twenty-seven years in prison, a sentence for the crime of believing that all people should have the same rights. Whites feared that when he was released he would bring about a violent change. They were amazed to hear him speak about reconciliation and the need to find roles for all of South Africa's citizens, including whites.

Mandela was born in 1918 in a small village in southeastern South Africa. His father was a leader of the Tembu people. Mandela attended the University of Fort Hare and later studied law. He and Oliver Tambo opened the first black law partnership in South Africa.

In his twenties, Mandela joined the African National Congress (ANC), a political organization that worked to overturn the nation's unjust laws. The white South

African government considered him a traitor because he spoke out against apartheid. The police hunted him down and he was brought to trial in 1961, charged with treason. Mandela became South Africa's most famous prisoner. Even from within the prison walls, he was able to influence other people. He communicated with young black leaders, helping them shape their ideas.

When he was released from prison, he made a remarkably fast entry into public life. In 1994, just four years after his release, Nelson Mandela was elected president of South Africa. Though Mandela is no longer president, his moral vision, his ideas, and his actions still guide the nation as it tackles its many problems.

in metal shacks without clean water. Millions who never had the chance at a good education do not have the skills to take part in a modern economy. South Africa needs thousands of trained teachers to improve the education system. For those South Africans who still live without decent housing, clean water, and electricity, waiting is difficult. Many have lost patience, and protests have become more common.

Still, South Africans can look with pride at all that has already been accomplished. The transformation of South Africa into a democratic, multiracial nation gives black South

In the years after apartheid ended, the government built millions of homes for poor South Africans, but millions more are still needed.

Africans a chance at a better life. At the same time, many of the nation's white citizens continue to enjoy considerable economic advantages. They are now recognized for what they really are: a minority group with a major role to play in the country's growth.

Today, South Africans of all races and cultures are free to vote and live where they want to. South Africans do business around the world and can compete in international sporting events. In 2010, South Africa hosted the World Cup, the world's premier soccer tournament, which is held only once every four years.

White South Africans make up less than 20 percent of the population of Cape Town.

South Africa built five new stadiums for the 2010 World Cup, including one in Cape Town.

Triumphant Tournament

The World Cup is one of the world's biggest sporting events. To prepare for hosting it, South Africa built stadiums all over the country and hotels to house the teams and the sports fans who flocked in from around the globe. The nation built new airports and improved roads. A million people attended the games in Cape Town, Johannesburg, Pretoria, Durban, Port Elizabeth, Nelspruit, Rustenburg, Polokwane, and Bloemfontein. Former president Mandela, who rarely makes public appearances, came out for the opening match that pitted South Africa against Mexico.

Although South Africa lost in the first round, the event was considered a huge success. During the tournament, the nation showed that it had world-class sports stadiums and transportation systems. It proved that other nations could depend on it to get the job done. This has brought South Africa investments from other countries and increased tourism, which are vital if the national economy is going to continue to grow. For young people in South Africa, the World Cup was proof that their nation was a respected member of the world community. It showed that South Africa was a modern nation, ready to invite the entire world to see the beauty of its land and the successful country it was building. Much still needs to be done, but uniting hundreds of thousands of people of all races for the World Cup is a landmark event in the nation's history.

Soccer fans packed stadiums across South Africa during the 2010 World Cup.

CHAPTER

TWO

From Sea
to Sea

THE REPUBLIC OF SOUTH AFRICA STRETCHES ACROSS the southernmost part of the African continent. The cold South Atlantic Ocean borders the west coast of the nation and wraps around the Cape of Good Hope peninsula. The warm Indian Ocean laps against the eastern and southern coasts, reaching a point called Cape Agulhas. The waters of the two oceans meet at this point, the southernmost point of the entire African continent. The village of Arniston on Cape Agulhas is the site of a boulder with a plaque that shows the Indian Ocean to the east and the South Atlantic Ocean to the west.

Opposite: **Waves lap upon the rocks at the Cape of Good Hope.**

The Lay of the Land

South Africa borders six nations. Namibia lies to the northwest, along the Orange River. The Molopo and Limpopo Rivers form part of the boundary separating South Africa from Botswana in the north. To the northeast is Zimbabwe, and to the east is Mozambique. The small mountainous nation of

South Africa's Geographic Features

Area: 471,359 square miles (1,220,814 sq km)

Highest Elevation: Njesuthi, 11,181 feet (3,408 m)

Lowest Elevation: Sea level along the coast

Longest River: Orange River, about 1,300 miles (2,100 km)

Most Southerly Point: Cape Agulhas

Length of Coastline: 1,836 miles (2,955 km)

Average High Temperature: In Johannesburg, 78°F (26°C) in January; 62°F (17°C) in July

Average Low Temperature: In Johannesburg, 59°F (15°C) in January; 39°F (4°C) in July

Average Annual Rainfall: 28 inches (71 cm) in Johannesburg; 20 inches (51 cm) in Cape Town

Lesotho, in the center-east, is surrounded entirely by South Africa. Swaziland, along the east coat, is almost completely surrounded by South Africa.

The Drakensberg is the tallest mountain range in southern Africa.

Along South Africa's long coastline is a narrow strip of flat land that rises up to form the dramatic Drakensberg mountain range in the eastern part of the country. The name, which means "dragon mountains" in Afrikaans, was inspired by the range's spiky peaks. Reaching heights of 11,000 feet (3,300 meters), they are the highest mountains in South Africa. In wintertime, there is snow on the tallest peaks, including Njesuthi, the nation's highest point at 11,181 feet (3,408 m).

In the western part of the country are the Cape Ranges. The Cederberg, Witsenberg, and Great Winterhoek Mountains run along the Atlantic Coast. The Swartberg and Langeberg Mountains rise near the southern coast.

Table Mountain

Table Mountain is the most recognizable mountain in South Africa. The mountain is well named. It rises dramatically and ends abruptly in a very flat top. When the air is moist, a cloud forms on the top of the mountain, spills over the sides, and then evaporates. This is called the "tablecloth." Table Mountain rises 3,563 feet (1,086 m) above the port city of Cape Town. It dominates the Cape of Good Hope peninsula and can be seen up to 100 miles (160 km) out at sea.

Thanks to the moisture provided by the tablecloth, Table Mountain has its own distinct zone of plants and flowers. More than 1,470 species of plants are found on the mountain. Many wild animals used to roam its slopes, but now only goats and small, furry creatures called rock hyraxes are found scampering over the rocks. A cable car runs to the top of Table Mountain. As the cable car runs up and down, it also rotates, giving visitors a spectacular view of the city of Cape Town and the harbor below.

About 200 miles (320 km) from the coast are arid plains called the Great Karoo and the Little Karoo. These grasslands get little rainfall. Some parts of the Karoo are suitable for grazing sheep and for ostrich ranching. Few towns are found there.

A high plateau occupies much of the interior of the nation. It has elevations of 2,000 to 8,000 feet (600 to 2,400 m) above sea level. Much of this land is rolling grassland with scattered trees.

One of South Africa's most unusual environments is found in the northwest. There, the climate seems to have a divided personality. At the very western edge of the land, icy cold winds blow onto the land from the Atlantic Ocean. They clash with the dry, hot air of the Namib Desert, which runs down the coast of Namibia, reaching into the northwest corner of South Africa. The contrast is so strong people feel hot and cold air on their bodies at the same time.

In the northwest region of South Africa lies Namaqualand. This desolate area seems barren and lifeless most of the year. Then, in spring, the region erupts into color as wildflowers blossom out of the dusty soil. This brilliant display lasts just a few weeks but it is considered one of South Africa's great natural wonders.

Spectacular wildflowers light up the landscape in Namaqualand.

Searching the Skies

The Karoo's brilliantly clear night skies have earned South Africa a prominent role in a project called the Square Kilometre Array, or SKA. When completed, SKA will be the world's largest radio telescope. It is designed to study how stars and galaxies form and change. The telescope requires a vast stretch of land with clear skies, no air pollution, and very little artificial light. The project is a joint venture between South Africa and Australia. Scientists will place thousands of receptors, extending 2,000 miles (3,000 km) from a central point. These will measure radio waves from space and produce the most detailed images in astronomy.

Climate

South Africa has a wide variety of climates. In many places, the winds blowing in from the ocean keep temperatures down in the summer. Some places can get extremely hot, however. The southwest has hot, dry summers, and temperatures soar in the Namib Desert in the extreme northwest. Parts of the central plateau are also extremely hot and dry. In winter, temperatures often drop below freezing in the mountains.

Some parts of northwestern South Africa are hot, desolate desert.

In most of the country, rainfall is more common in the summer. But the southwest of the country experiences cool, damp winters.

Snow blankets a fruit tree orchard in the western part of South Africa.

Powering the Future

South Africa has a large population and a growing need for electricity. The government is searching for ways to supply this demand. The nation gets some of its energy from a nuclear power plant, and the national energy company has proposed building more.

One of the most controversial ideas for supplying electricity is a process called hydraulic fracturing, or fracking, which breaks up a layer of rock in the earth to reach oil or natural gas below it. Fracking requires enormous amounts of water for each well that is dug. In the Karoo, the region of South Africa where fracking is being considered, water is extremely scarce. Sheep

Large wind turbines rise from a field near Cape Town.

farmers in the vast, desolate region sometimes have to slaughter their animals because there isn't enough rainfall to keep them alive. These farmers are opposed to fracking.

The government, however, believes it can create jobs and provide the nation with energy from natural gas buried deep below the surface. Shell, the company that has proposed drilling in South Africa, plans to drill exploratory wells to see how much gas can be found. If the results are positive, the company expects to drill at least 1,500 wells.

Many farmers would prefer that the government promote solar power or wind power. These types of energy are in endless supply, and using them doesn't damage the environment. South Africa has abundant sunshine, especially in the Karoo, where the sky is bright year-round. Wind power is already being used in the Western Cape Province, in the southwest of the country. Thanks to the strong winds that blow in from the Atlantic Ocean, it is a good place to install large wind turbines, which generate electricity as they turn. Although wind is free, it costs money to set up the equipment and use it. In the future, South Africa expects to generate enough electricity from wind turbines to supply part of Cape Town's needs.

Looking at South Africa's Cities

With a population of more than 3.6 million, Johannesburg (below) is South Africa's largest city and the heart of the nation's economic activity. It is known as Egoli, a Zulu word that means "place of gold," because it was built atop the gold mines that gave South Africa its great wealth. Johannesburg is one of the liveliest cities in the nation. Its arts and cultural activities are centered on the old Market Theatre in the Newtown district. Museum Africa brings the nation's history to life with interactive exhibits. Visitors who take the elevator to the top of the Carlton Centre Office Tower get a 360-degree view of the city. The Nelson Mandela Bridge, opened in 2003, connects two areas of Johannesburg: Braamfontein and Newtown. The bridge was a complicated construction project, crossing more than forty railway lines.

Cape Town, South Africa's second-largest city with a population of about 3.3 million, is the nation's legislative capital. Ekurhuleni, also known as East Rand, is the

nation's third-largest city, with a population of about 3.1 million. It is part of the greater Johannesburg area. East Rand includes many black townships that experienced heavy fighting during the struggle to end apartheid.

Durban (above), on the Indian Ocean, is South Africa's largest port and fourth-largest city, home to more than 2.8 million people. This bustling city reflects the country's past and present in its ethnic mix and its vibrant economy. Durban was founded in 1835 and named for Sir Benjamin D'Urban, a British general and governor of the Cape Colony. In the nineteenth century, the owners of sugar plantations brought in many workers from India. Today, black Zulus outnumber Indians in Durban, but the city retains a distinctly Indian flavor. Durban is extremely hot and humid in the summer. In the winter, however, it attracts many visitors from Cape Town and Johannesburg seeking to escape the windy winter weather at home to relax on Durban's warm, sunny beaches. Visitors also enjoy the uShaka Marine World Park, which offers a look at underwater sea life. The park includes a model of a wrecked 1920s cargo ship, giving a sense of the danger involved navigating around South Africa's coasts.

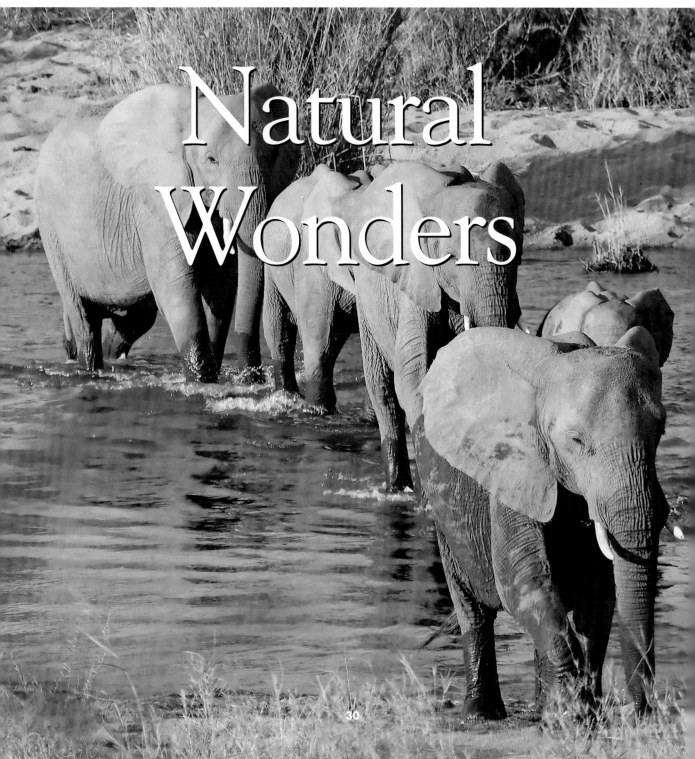

Natural Wonders

FROM DIGNIFIED ELEPHANTS GRAZING IN THE GRASSLANDS to powerful whales leaping out of the water, South Africa is home to many majestic animals. About three hundred different species of mammals live in South Africa. Many visitors travel to South Africa to see the "big five": elephants, buffaloes, lions, leopards, and rhinoceroses. But the country is also home to many other magnificent species of animals.

Many types of antelope are found in South Africa, including oryx, gazelles, gemsboks, impalas, waterbucks, and elands. Each has distinctive horns and markings that make them easy to tell apart. The tallest mammals on earth, giraffes, are very easy to spot, as are zebras, with their sharp black and white stripes. Interestingly, the markings on both giraffes and zebras are different on each individual animal, like fingerprints are on humans.

Opposite: **Elephants in Kruger National Park. Elephants live in large family groups of adult females and their children.**

The Springbok

The springbok is a small antelope unique to South Africa. The springbok stands about 30 inches (75 centimeters) high and weighs about 90 pounds (40 kilograms). The springbok got its name because of its ability to leap far and high. This makes it the perfect choice as the symbol of South Africa's rugby team, called the Springboks.

During the transition away from apartheid, some people thought the country should choose a new symbol because the springbok was identified with white rugby players. Then, at the 1995 Rugby World Cup final held in South Africa, President Nelson Mandela wore a green springbok jersey while congratulating the winning South African team captain. The crowd went wild, and the springbok symbol stuck.

The Whale Coast

A short drive from Cape Town is the town of Hermanus on Walker Bay. It is the most important site for whale watchers in South Africa. During the migrating season that stretches from May to November, southern right whales begin arriving in Walker Bay. The whales migrate from Antarctica to the warm waters of this protected inlet to give birth and nurse their young.

The town of Hermanus is perched high up on a cliff where people gather for a good view of the whales below. When whales are spotted, a "whale crier" announces their arrival. There is even a whale hotline, a telephone number people can call to find out if whales have been spotted that day.

Many other creatures also live in these waters. Sharks are common. They find plenty to eat here, including Cape fur seals that make their home on Dyker Island, not far from Cape Town. Shark sightseeing boats take visitors to see the sharks. Some of these tour guides engage in a practice called chumming. They bait the sharks by tossing chum, or fish guts, into the water. On some trips, visitors enter the water in metal cages, so they can have a close-up view of sharks. Wildlife conservationists are against these activities. They are dangerous and interfere with the sharks' normal habits.

Bothered by Baboons

South Africa is home to many types of monkeys. One species has become an environmental problem. The Chacma baboon, or Cape baboon, is among the largest of monkey species, weighing up to 68 pounds (31

kg). The baboons, which travel in troops of a dozen or more, have grown used to living around houses and people in the Constantia suburb, near Cape Town. They are also found in packs in the Cape of Good Hope Nature Reserve. As baboons come into contact with people, they grow bold. These baboons now associate humans with food, and they sometimes invade homes in search of a meal. They are clever at opening doors and lifting lids from garbage cans. It is estimated that three hundred baboons make their home in the Cape of Good Hope Nature Reserve. A group called the Baboon Matters Trust works to protect the baboons. They sometimes relocate animals that have moved into areas populated by people.

South Africa is one of the best birding locations in the world. More than 850 different bird species have been recorded in the country. About fifty species are found only in South Africa. Migrating birds arrive from as far away as the Arctic, Central Asia, and Antarctica.

Each area of South Africa is home to different species of birds. The province of KwaZulu-Natal, in the east of the country, has an incredibly rich bird population. The warm climate is just right for many species, including the Woodward's barbet, the African broadbill, the crowned eagle, and various species of turacos and sunbirds.

Turacos eat mainly fruit. They are noted for their brightly colored feathers.

The number of African penguins is dropping dramatically. In the year 2000, their population was about two hundred thousand. By 2010, the penguin population had dropped to fifty-five thousand.

Different species are seen in West Coast National Park, along the Langebaan Lagoon. Here, wading birds just in from the Arctic are common. These include the curlew sandpiper and the black harrier.

Perhaps the most easily recognized birds in South Africa are ones that don't actually fly. Penguins live along much of the South African coast. These are the African penguins, also called jackass penguins because of their braying call. African penguins are quite small, standing about 27 inches high (70 cm) and weighing between 5 and 11 pounds (2 and 5 kg). It is quite a sight to see these little penguins waddling across a parking lot on their way to the beach. Near a place called the Boulders, the penguins have become very used to people. Penguins and people share the beach. The penguins allow people to come nearly within arm's reach before they walk away or head for the ocean where they feed on the fish.

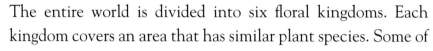

A wide variety of plants and flowers grow in the Cape Floral Region.

The entire world is divided into six floral kingdoms. Each kingdom covers an area that has similar plant species. Some of these kingdoms are vast. The same floral kingdom, for example, covers most of North America, Asia, and all of Europe. The smallest floral kingdom by far is the Cape Floral Region, which covers only the southern tip of South Africa. Though small, it boasts remarkable diversity. More than 9,000 species of plants grow there, and about 6,200 of them occur nowhere else in the world. More than 2,000 different species of plants grow on Table Mountain alone, adding to the mountain's reputation as one of the most interesting and beautiful parts of South Africa. These include the king protea (the national flower) and the silver tree, an evergreen with thick, silky, silver leaves.

Other notable plants grow elsewhere in South Africa. The marula tree produces large fruits that are favorites of elephants. A marula tree has a thick trunk and a wide

World Heritage Sites

The Cape Floral Region was declared a World Heritage Site in 2004. It is one of eight such sites in South Africa. These sites are places of unusual importance and are in need of protection. If they should disappear through neglect or overuse they cannot be brought back to life. World Heritage Sites are determined by the United Nations Educational, Scientific and Cultural Organization (UNESCO), a part of the United Nations.

Greater St. Lucia Wetland Park was named a World Heritage Site in 1999. It was added to the list because of its exceptional variety of species, its coral reefs, and its coastal dunes. That same year, UNESCO added fossil sites in the Sterkfontein area, where the remains of

the earliest human beings have been found. These fossils trace human ancestors back 3.5 million years. The uKhahlamba-Drakensberg Park was named a World Heritage Site to protect caves that the San people covered with paintings roughly thirty thousand years ago. The Vredefort Dome, the world's largest meteorite impact site, was added to the list in 2005. A World Heritage Site can also be a place of political importance. Robben Island, where Nelson Mandela was held prisoner for many years, is a World Heritage Site.

Mapungubwe National Park, the site of one of the earliest kingdoms in Africa, was named a World Heritage Site in 2003. This site is located where South Africa, Zimbabwe, and Botswana meet. Gold objects, including the rhinoceros shown above, were found at the site and show that skilled artisans lived there by about 1000 CE. Rock paintings show that Khoi and San people lived there even earlier. The park includes a museum housing the objects found at the site.

In 2007, Richtersveld Cultural and Botanical Landscape (left) became the latest addition to the list of World Heritage sites in South Africa. Richtersveld is a rugged landscape that is the home of the Nama people, traditional herders who move with the seasons.

The National Flower

The dramatic king protea is South Africa's national flower. This unusual flower is huge. The flower head measures 12 inches (30 cm) across and sports a circle of spiky petals. It grows throughout the southwestern and southern parts of South Africa.

The kokerboom tree is an unusual plant that grows in Namaqualand. It can store a lot of water in its branches, allowing it to thrive in the dry land.

canopy. These trees are often used as meeting sites in villages. Some groups in South Africa use the bark in medicines. It is used to treat stomach ailments, insect bites, and other health problems.

National Parks and Reserves

South Africa has established many wildlife reserves to protect the nation's animal population. South Africa created its national park system in 1926, when it established Kruger National Park. Kruger lies in the northern part of the country near Zimbabwe and Mozambique. It is one of the largest wildlife reserves in Africa, covering 7,523 square miles (19,485 square kilometers). That's larger than the U.S. state of Connecticut. Another popular national park is Addo Elephant Park on the southeastern coast. It is home to more than 450 elephants.

Rhinoceroses in Kruger National Park. Rhino horns are made of keratin, the same material that makes up hair and fingernails.

Gemsboks are one of the many animals that live in Kgalagadi Transfrontier Park. Both male and female gemsboks have long, thin horns.

There are currently twenty parks in the South African national park system. Park management continues to add land to the parks to protect wildlife, marine life, and plants.

The country is also joining with other nations to form larger wildlife reserves. Many animals migrate as the seasons change, seeking better supplies of food and water. Often, they come up against fences that separate wildlife reserves in two nations. Unable to continue along their traditional migration routes, many animals die.

After long negotiations, South Africa entered into an agreement with the country of Botswana to create a transfrontier park.

A frontier is another word for a border. This new park is called Kgalagadi Transfrontier Park, named for a group of people that settled in the area long ago. It allows wildlife to move freely between the two nations. Two local communities have joined with the South African government to govern the land in the best interests of the wildlife. This new park is twice the size of Kruger National Park.

South Africa has also been involved in the formation of a second transfrontier park. Together with Zimbabwe and Mozambique, it created an enormous wildlife area called the Great Limpopo Transfrontier Park. It links Kruger National Park with Gonarezhou National Park in Zimbabwe and Limpopo National Park in Mozambique.

About 1,600 lions live in Kruger National Park.

The Poaching Problem

South African animals face many threats. Poaching, or illegal hunting, is one of the greatest threats. In recent years, there have been many bloody attacks on rhinoceroses. The poachers aren't interested in the whole animal—they only want the rhinoceros's horns—but to get the horn, they must kill the rhino. The poachers sell the rhinoceros horns in the Asian nations of Vietnam and China, where some people believe the horns can cure cancer. This isn't true, but it hasn't stopped the attacks. Poachers typically kill more than three hundred rhinoceroses each year. This is a dangerous business for everyone involved. Each year in South Africa, park rangers trying to protect the wildlife kill poachers, and poachers kill some of the rangers protecting the animals.

Ancient and Modern

S OUTH AFRICA IS KNOWN AS THE CRADLE OF Humankind. Fossils from four different species of hominids— our ancient ancestors—have been found in caves there dating back 3.5 million years. The first scientific discovery of early human life was made in 1924 in northwestern South Africa. A skull, now known as the Taung Child, was unearthed there. It changed scientists' ideas about where human life began. Today, visitors can explore limestone caves in the province of KwaZulu-Natal where some of these discoveries were made and where fossils are still being unearthed today.

Opposite: **Thousands of years ago, the San people made paintings on cave walls in what is now South Africa.**

Early Settlers

The first modern human beings to live in South Africa were hunter-gatherers. They were skilled at hunting animals. They also gathered food from the plants they found. Evidence of the way they lived is found in their cave and rock paintings. These paintings show the animals that lived in the region at that time.

Today, these people are called the San. They have been living in Africa for about thirty thousand years. Although most San now live in the neighboring countries of Namibia and Botswana, small communities of San remain in South Africa.

Over thousands of years, people migrated around southern Africa. Sometimes they moved as the climate changed. Some moved to find new grazing land.

A major change in South Africa's population began around 300 CE when Bantu-speaking people began arriving in the eastern part of the country from much farther north. They established communities and became farmers. They also

The San were the first people to live in what is now South Africa. Today, a few thousand San still live in the country.

raised livestock. The Bantu were the first people to make use of the metals found in the area, including copper, iron, and gold. They became skilled at working these metals, which they used as trade goods. Most of today's black South Africans are descended from these Bantu people.

About 1,200 years ago, the Khoikhoi people moved into southern Africa from farther north. They settled in groups, raising sheep and cattle, and hunting and gathering.

Traditionally, the Khoikhoi lived in round huts. The framework of the huts was made from bent green branches that were then covered with mats made of reeds.

Europeans Arrive

Portuguese explorer Bartolomeu Dias led the first European expedition to reach South Africa. His ship arrived on the southern coast in 1488. It was not until 1652 that Europeans landed and remained in South Africa. That was the year that Captain Jan van Riebeeck, sailing for the Dutch East

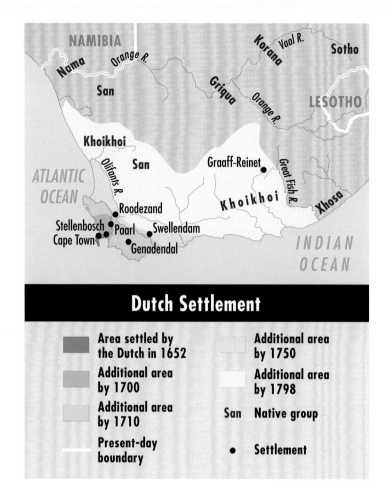

Dutch Settlement

Area settled by the Dutch in 1652	Additional area by 1750
Additional area by 1700	Additional area by 1798
Additional area by 1710	San Native group
Present-day boundary	• Settlement

India Company, arrived from Holland. His task was to establish a food supply stop for the company's ships as they made their way around the Cape of Good Hope. His crew established a garden. It still exists today in Cape Town, in back of the Houses of Parliament.

The Dutch settled in the region that would become Cape Town and the Cape Colony. The arrival of the Dutch marked the beginning of modern South Africa. It also set the stage for the multiracial country that developed. Some Dutch sailors had children with black Khoikhoi women. In South Africa, these and other mixed-race children became known as Coloureds.

The Dutch were followed by shiploads of Huguenots, Protestants who had left France to find religious freedom. German settlers also soon arrived in southern Africa. Together, these three European groups and their black servants began to create a new language similar to Dutch that would become known as Afrikaans. Those who migrated into the interior of South Africa were known as Boers, the Dutch word for "farmers." In the late nineteenth century, they began to call themselves Afrikaners, "people of Africa."

Some of the white settlers mixed with the local black people, but Captain Jan van Riebeeck had already set South Africa on a path in which the races were separated. He and his men traded with the Khoikhoi and San people, exchanging metal products and tobacco for cattle, sheep, and goats, but he had a fort built to protect his men and his family from these groups.

The Dutch in South Africa built several windmills, which they used to grind grain.

Ancient and Modern **47**

The Xhosa, a Bantu people, traditionally lived in the southeastern part of South Africa.

As the settlement grew, some of his men left to establish their own community in the region where the Khoikhoi lived. The Khoikhoi did not believe in land ownership. Instead, they thought that the land was there to be used by everyone. However, the Europeans did believe in land ownership. Van Riebeeck pushed the Khoikhoi out, making them trespassers on their own land. When the Dutch company decided to establish farms to grow food for their small community, they brought in people from southeastern Africa as well as people from different parts of Asia and enslaved them.

As the white population along the coast grew, settlements began to spread into the interior. In the late 1770s, as some Boers migrated farther inland and to the east, they encountered the Xhosa people. The Xhosa and other Africans lived in communities that were ruled by traditional chiefs. Many battles took place between the Boers and the Xhosa.

By this time, Cape Town had grown into a busy seaport. It was an appealing base for other Europeans. In the late 1700s, France invaded Holland, and Dutch power was fading. In 1795, the Dutch invited the British to take over the Cape colony to prevent the French from seizing it.

Shaka Leads the Zulus

By the 1800s, Zulu people were living along the eastern part of South Africa near the Indian Ocean. In 1816, a brilliant military man named Shaka came to power as chief of his people. He quickly built up his army to a force of two thousand highly disciplined warriors. He devised a new method of fighting with a short, stabbing spear called an *itlwa*. He also devised a new way of positioning his army regiments so they surrounded and closed in on an enemy. Using these two techniques, Shaka and his men defeated other kingdoms. The Zulu kingdom grew into the largest in all of southern Africa. Shaka ruled for just thirteen years, but his influence on South Africa is still felt in Zululand. The Zulus are proud of their warrior history. The president of modern South Africa, Jacob Zuma, is a member of the Zulu people.

The first British to arrive were followed by a larger group known as the 1820 Settlers, who formed the base of the English-speaking population. The British and Dutch fought over differences in language and culture. Meanwhile, the Boers were fighting the black African kingdoms. Some of these kingdoms were also fighting one another.

The Great Trek

On December 1, 1834, the British outlawed slavery in South Africa. Some Boers decided to get away from these laws and they embarked on what became known as the Great Trek. They loaded all their possessions onto ox-drawn wagons and made the hard journey over the Drakensberg Mountains. Although they were now far away from the British, this move brought them to lands where other Bantu-speaking people lived. They found themselves fighting against the Zulus, who were powerful and determined fighters. The Boers and the Zulus fought many battles in the 1830s. In 1838, the Boers won a major victory at the Battle of Blood River. This was the beginning of the white conquest of the eastern half of South Africa.

The Zulu Kingdom

- Shaka's Zulu kingdom in 1817
- Zulu lands before Shaka
- Main Boer trek route, 1835–1854
- Battle between Zulus and Boers
- Battle between Zulus and English
- Settlement
- Present-day boundary

Map labels: Pretoria, Johannesburg, Vaal R., Vegkop (1836), Komatipoort, SWAZILAND, Maputo R., Isandlwana (1879), Ulundi (1879), Rorke's Drift (1879), Ladysmith, Umfolozi R., Tugela R., Orange R., Weenen, INDIAN OCEAN, LESOTHO, Pietermaritzburg, Durban

Cecil Rhodes

Cecil Rhodes was an Englishman with grand dreams. He wanted the British to control all of Africa, and he wanted to build a railroad that would run the length of the continent. He never completed his railroad across the continent but he became a powerful figure in South Africa.

Rhodes had a knack for making money. In 1870, he left England for South Africa to improve his health. Hearing about the diamond mines, he settled in the diamond-mining town of Kimberley and began buying up small mining claims. In 1888, he and one of his rivals formed De Beers Consolidated Mines, which was named for the farm where diamonds were found. Rhodes soon controlled most of South Africa's diamond-mining industry and had an important stake in gold mining. De Beers remains the most important diamond company in the world.

Fighting over Minerals

The Afrikaners wanted to live apart from other people and establish their own independent states. The land they wanted for farming proved later to hold much of South Africa's great mineral wealth. Diamonds were discovered in 1867, near the Orange River in what is now central South Africa. This area was claimed by the Boers, the British, and African groups.

In 1886, a large deposit of gold was discovered in an area known as the Witwatersrand. Gold and diamonds would shape the future of South Africa. They made a few men very rich. Some miners came from nearby communities, but many hundreds of thousands came from more distant places such as Mozambique and Lesotho.

The British and the Afrikaners battled for control of southern Africa at the end of the nineteenth century.

The British looked upon the Afrikaners as poor farmers who were standing in their way of making the most of the gold that lay underground. In 1881, the first Anglo-Boer War broke out. The Second Boer War started in 1899. The battles raged on and off until 1902. By the time the fighting was over, the British had brought in 448,000 soldiers—five times the number of Afrikaners who had fought.

The Union of South Africa

By the early twentieth century, Great Britain controlled much of the land that makes up what is now South Africa. In 1910, Britain brought together four of the colonies in the region— Natal, Free State, Orange, and Transvaal—to form the Union of South Africa. Full citizenship was limited mostly to whites. A small number of blacks and Coloureds in the Cape had the right to vote, but the vast majority of blacks were denied the vote. In 1912, black South Africans created the African National Congress (ANC) to fight for full citizenship.

The land's white rulers legalized the separation of whites and blacks. In 1913, they enacted the Natives' Land Act. This act restricted the areas of land that could be owned by black South Africans, who were referred to as "natives." Blacks were not allowed to own land in most of the country, including all of the cities. These were declared to be for the exclusive use of whites.

The group that would become the African National Congress first met in Bloemfontein in 1912.

Blacks could only enter the cities to work for whites. Otherwise, they were confined to crowded black townships. In 1936, whites controlled 93 percent of the land. They passed laws that eventually provided 13 percent of the land to blacks, who outnumbered whites by seven to one. The land that blacks were allowed to own was the least useful: it was the worst for growing crops.

Conditions for black South Africans worsened in the 1920s and 1930s. As laws were put into place limiting what they could do and where they could live, they had fewer

Gold miners work in a mine near Johannesburg in 1935.

White South Africans relax at a hotel in Cape Town in the 1930s. Blacks were not allowed there.

opportunities. Life was getting harder, both for black farmers working on land owned by whites and for people crowded into slums. In the 1920s, the Industrial and Commercial Workers' Union, a black political organization, protested against the difficult conditions. Its members called for land for rural blacks and greater freedom for everyone.

Establishing Apartheid

In 1948, the National Party, which represented the Afrikaners, won the general election. This party quickly set about enacting laws to separate all the people in South Africa according to ethnic background. This was called *apartheid*, a word that means separateness. Apartheid was intended to separate the races in every aspect of daily life. Beaches, park benches, and water fountains were segregated. Blacks were forced to

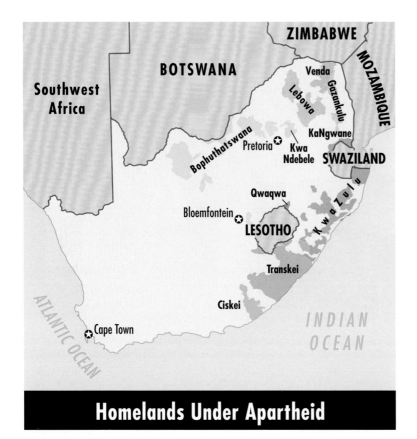

Homelands Under Apartheid

use separate doors to enter post offices, banks, and other buildings. Apartheid established rules for where black people could live, go to school, get medical care, and work. Blacks had to carry passes to prove they had a job and a legal right to be in a city. They also had to prove they had the right to live in a particular township. The Afrikaners wanted to know exactly where all black South Africans lived.

The effort to promote the interest of Afrikaners and limit the rights of others was led by the National Party leader, Prime Minister Hendrik Verwoerd. He ruled the nation from 1958 until he was assassinated in 1966. He set in motion two policies meant to raise whites above blacks in every aspect of life. Even today, South Africans are dealing with the lasting impact of his policies.

One of those policies was the idea of "homelands." All black South Africans were assigned to one of ten regions within South Africa. Blacks without jobs, even temporarily, were supposed to go "home" to a homeland, even if they had never been there before. According to Verwoerd, black Africans were not citizens of South Africa; they belonged in these homelands.

Verwoerd also promoted a system called Bantu Education, which limited the subjects taught to black Africans. They were not allowed to learn math, science, and many other subjects. Verwoerd thought blacks were suitable only for working as laborers and maids, so they had no need to be educated in such subjects.

Opposition to Apartheid

Black political parties organized protests against apartheid laws. The African National Congress (ANC), under the leadership of Nelson Mandela, Walter Sisulu, and Oliver Tambo, led protests and strikes. In 1952, the ANC, the South African Indian Congress, and the Coloured People's Congress planned a defiance campaign. People would peacefully defy unfair laws, hoping that the government would be unable to deal with all the arrests it would be forced to make. Thousands of people were arrested for breaking the curfew for blacks or walking through entrances to buildings reserved for whites. The defiance campaign gained a lot of attention, and membership in the ANC grew from seven thousand to one hundred thousand.

Hendrik Verwoerd is remembered for establishing many apartheid policies.

Forced Removals

The government forced millions of blacks to move from their homes to fulfill the policy of racial separation. Black South Africans did not want to leave the neighborhoods they lived in. Those who did not move voluntarily were forced out. In 1955, the lively area of Sophiatown in Johannesburg was emptied of its residents. The houses, bars, and nightclubs where blacks gathered were torn down to make way for the new white area called Triomf (which means "triumph" in Afrikaans).

In 1966, the government tore into an area called District Six (above) in the heart of Cape Town. This section of Cape Town was offensive to the nation's white leaders. It was close to City Hall, close to Parliament, close to the city's business center. Every day, the members of parliament saw how the people of District Six defied the whole idea of apartheid. The residents of District Six were of all races and religions. Most were Coloureds, but blacks and whites lived in this vibrant community as well. This was not the way the National Party believed things should be.

The government declared District Six "white." Shortly thereafter, police came in the middle of the night and removed some blacks who lived in the neighborhood. Neighbors woke up the next day and found empty houses and apartments where those people had lived.

Between 1968 and 1982, the government forced sixty thousand people out of their homes in District Six. People and their belongings were simply tossed out on the street. Some people were taken by truck to the remote Cape Flats, where they were divided according to their race. Others were left on the sidewalk with nowhere to go.

Once the people were gone, bulldozers moved in and reduced the houses to rubble. The plan was to build new houses for white people. But the shame of what had been done was so great that no one wanted to live in this area. The streets remained empty. No houses were ever built.

Years later, plans were announced to create homes for five thousand people and to give them to the former residents of District Six if they could prove they once lived there. In 2004, some houses were completed, and Nelson Mandela welcomed the first returning residents to District Six.

In 1959, some members of the ANC left the organization and formed the Pan-Africanist Congress (PAC). They believed that the ANC should not be working so closely with white groups in the struggle for black liberation. The PAC also organized defiance of apartheid laws.

As demonstrations grew in strength, the government responded harshly. On April 8, 1960, it banned the ANC and the PAC, making it a crime to be a member of these organizations. Some of the leaders of these groups went into hiding but continued to work against apartheid. Nelson Mandela, the best-

Taxis were among the many services that were segregated in South Africa during the apartheid era.

known South African leader, did this. Eventually, he was found and tried for treason. In 1964, he was sentenced to life in prison. Other leaders of the movement fled the country, organizing the fight against apartheid from friendly nations. Thabo Mbeki, who became South Africa's president after Nelson Mandela retired, fled the country to fight the apartheid system from elsewhere. He remained out of the country for nearly thirty years.

Thabo Mbeki lived in the country of Zambia for many years. From there, he served as the ANC's director of publicity and information.

With tremendous force, the government attacked any-one resisting apartheid. The police and the army were called upon every time blacks rose up against the apartheid laws. On March 21, 1960, a group of unarmed blacks went to the police station in the black township of Sharpeville to hold a peaceful protest against the passbook laws. All black South Africans had to carry a passbook to travel or work. In Sharpeville that day, thousands of demonstrators left their passbooks at home, expecting to be arrested. The police responded to the demonstration with gunfire. By the time the shooting was over, sixty-nine blacks were dead. Many had been shot in the back as they tried to flee when the shooting began. Their deaths sparked a nationwide protest.

Wounded people lie in the street after the police opened fire in Sharpeville. More than two hundred people were injured or killed in the massacre.

Steve Biko (right) helped inspire student protests in 1976.

Despite the government's harsh reaction to protests, black South Africans continued to struggle to bring about change. At first, the ANC had not accepted white members. But by the late 1960s, whites were allowed to join its ranks. In 1968, students founded the South African Students' Organization (SASO), with Steve Biko as its president. Biko and other members of SASO believed that only blacks could fight for their own freedom, so only blacks were allowed to join. But the organization used a different definition of "black" than was normal in South Africa. Biko and the other members of SASO considered anyone who was oppressed by the apartheid system—whether African, Indian, or Coloured—to be black.

Then, in 1976, black students rose up in fury against a new government policy on language. While students were usually taught in their ethnic language in primary school, in high school some subjects were taught in other languages. Black students wanted to be taught in English, a language in general use. The government insisted they be taught in Afrikaans instead. The black students viewed Afrikaans as the language of their oppressors and the apartheid system. They staged a protest march in the black township of Soweto near Johannesburg on June 16. Thousands of students boycotted classes and took to the streets.

Two young people in Soweto kneel in front of the police during language protests in 1976. About twenty thousand students took part in the protests.

The police were called in to put down the protest. The soldiers were ordered to fire at the unarmed crowd. Hector Pieterson, a thirteen-year-old boy, was killed, and several other people were wounded. Protests rippled across the country. In the next few months, more than six hundred protesters, many of them children, were killed. The protests and the brutality were seen around the world. The government continued to use violent force against anyone who tried to lead a protest. Steve Biko was tortured and ultimately murdered by the police while in custody in 1977.

Youth Day honors young people who died in the struggle against apartheid. On Youth Day, flowers are laid at a memorial to Hector Pieterson, who was killed in the Soweto uprising.

As minister of justice, B. J. Vorster brutally put down opposition to apartheid. He oversaw the trial that sentenced Nelson Mandela to life in prison and was prime minister during the Soweto protests.

June 16 is now celebrated in South Africa as Youth Day, in honor of the students who risked their lives that day in Soweto in 1976.

Outside Pressure

B. J. Vorster served as prime minister from 1966 to 1978. Vorster softened some minor rules of apartheid, such as one that designated "whites-only" entrances to buildings and laws that prohibited marriage between whites and blacks. But he left the main elements of apartheid in place.

In the 1970s and 1980s, students and citizens around the world began protests demanding that companies not do business in South Africa or support South Africa financially in any way. In 1987, Columbia University in New York City, urged on by the students there, pulled all its investments out of South Africa. This encouraged other institutions to do the same. The burden of apartheid was now financial as well as moral.

The End of Apartheid

P. W. Botha, who had been prime minister of South Africa from 1978 to 1984, took office as the first state president in 1984. By then, with unrest at home and pressure from around the world, it was clear that apartheid had to end. Botha was unable to make the changes that were needed, however, and was forced to resign in 1989. F. W. de Klerk replaced him. Although de Klerk was an Afrikaner and loyal to the National

P. W. Botha favored continuing apartheid.

The Apartheid Museum

The Apartheid Museum in Johannesburg offers a powerful reminder of South Africa's bitter history. Visitors to the museum, which opened in 2001, buy tickets that indicate they are either "white" or "non-white." The museum preserves many artifacts of apartheid including passbooks and prison cages. It illustrates the rise and fall of apartheid using many dramatic and emotional displays.

Party, he saw that the majority of the population could not be denied their rights forever.

De Klerk understood that the only way to end apartheid was to talk with the leaders of the ANC. On February 2, 1990, de Klerk announced that the ANC, the PAC, and other organizations representing blacks were no longer illegal. A few days later, on February 11, 1990, Nelson Mandela was released from prison after twenty-seven years.

F. W. de Klerk had to make sure that his fellow white South Africans were ready for the monumental changes needed to end apartheid. On March 17, 1992, the white population voted on a single question, essentially asking people if they were willing to end white rule in South Africa. More than two-thirds of the voters answered "Yes."

De Klerk will always be remembered as the man who released Nelson Mandela from prison and paved the way for South Africa to have its first black president. Conservative Afrikaners see de Klerk as a traitor. But to most South Africans, including many Afrikaners, he had made an honorable decision. De Klerk and Mandela were jointly awarded the Nobel Peace Prize in 1993 for their work in ending apartheid peacefully.

Nelson Mandela and F. W. de Klerk celebrate the passage of South Africa's new, democratic constitution in 1996.

Forgiveness

In 1995, the South African government appointed a Truth and Reconciliation Commission to look into the crimes committed during apartheid. Archbishop Desmond Tutu (right), a civil rights leader and Anglican priest, was chosen to head the commission. His second in command, Alex Boraine, served as an opposition member of Parliament for more than a decade.

South Africa's former white rulers, the police, and the army had committed many acts of violence against antiapartheid protesters. Some people trying to end apartheid had also committed atrocities. The South African government created the commission to find a way to bring former enemies together. People who wanted to confess to crimes they had committed could appear before the committee and face members of the family involved.

In 1995, the commission began two years of hearings. Archbishop Tutu and the other commission members heard horrible tales of violence and an outpouring of sorrow and grief. They believed that the stories needed to be heard before forgiveness could begin and South Africa could start to heal and move forward.

Beyond Apartheid

De Klerk and Mandela engaged in long, difficult negotiations about the future of South Africa. To begin, blacks were given full citizenship rights. Everyone who was at least eighteen years old could vote.

South Africa's first democratic elections were held in April 1994. Millions of people voted for the first time in their lives. People waited in the hot sun for hours, sometimes all day, to cast that first ballot.

South Africans stood in line for hours to vote in the general election in 1994. It was the first election in which all adult South Africans could take part, regardless of their race.

The ANC won the elections easily, and Nelson Mandela was chosen to be South Africa's first black president. He took over a country facing desperate problems, but filled with hope for the future.

Into the Twenty-First Century

When Mandela's presidential term ended in 1999, he chose not to run for a second term. He believed the best example he could set for the young democracy was to prepare the people for a regular transfer of power decided at the election booth.

The new leader of the ANC, Thabo Mbeki, was elected president in 1999. He was reelected in 2004 but resigned in 2008 when he lost the support of the ANC.

As South Africa matures, it must face the difficult task of ruling a nation that is modern and technologically advanced but also has a large, poorly educated rural population. Corruption has also taken hold in many areas of public life. Inexperience and greed, for example, led to the Limpopo Province spending itself into bankruptcy. The business of that province was taken over by the national government.

Jacob Zuma was elected president in 2009. He must find a way to satisfy the growing demands of the people for better housing, better sanitation, better schools, and more jobs. After nearly twenty years as a democratic nation, South Africa finds itself needing to catch up following centuries of inequality.

Orania, the Afrikaner Town

When apartheid ended and South Africa elected its first black president, a number of Afrikaners refused to accept their changed status. They believed fervently in the idea of separation of the races. Unlike the previous white-ruled government, however, they believed in a total separation, one in which whites did not depend on the labor of blacks. In 1990, a group of about forty Afrikaner families purchased a deserted town located along the Orange River in the Karoo. They established a new town based on the ideas of a company in which the residents buy shares. Then they set about to create a new, all-white society that they called Orania. Their leader was Carel Boshoff, the son-in-law of Hendrik Verwoerd, the man most closely identified with apartheid. Only people who believe in the Afrikaner culture may live there. The whites are completely self-sufficient and perform all the jobs necessary to keep the town going. By 2012, their population had increased to about one thousand.

Starting Over

IT IS EXTREMELY RARE FOR AN ESTABLISHED NATION to create an entirely new form of government. That was the unusual task facing South Africa as it became a nonracial democracy. The process began on May 10, 1994, after the elections and the new members of government were sworn in.

They began by writing a new constitution, basic laws that established how the people would be governed. They took the idea of a bill of rights from the U.S. Constitution and made it part of their own. The rights guaranteed by the South African constitution go far beyond those in the United States. These include the right to a healthy environment, and the rights to housing, health care, food, water, and education.

It took more than two years to write the document. President Mandela signed the new constitution into law on December 10, 1996, at Sharpeville. He chose to sign the constitution there as a way of honoring a pledge to guarantee personal freedom for all South Africans and to remember those who lost their lives fighting for that freedom.

Opposite: **A South African votes in an election in Johannesburg. South Africans must be eighteen years old to vote.**

Jacob Zuma

Jacob Zuma was elected president on May 6, 2009. Like Nelson Mandela, he had spent years in prison on Robben Island for his role in fighting apartheid, and he later lived in exile in various countries. Unlike Mandela, he had no formal education. In spite of this, he became a leader in the African National Congress and then president.

Running the Government

As in the United States, the president of South Africa is both the head of state and the head of government. He or she is chosen by members of Parliament and serves a five-year term. The president is allowed to serve two terms. The president is assisted by a cabi-

The National Assembly meets in the Houses of Parliament in Cape Town.

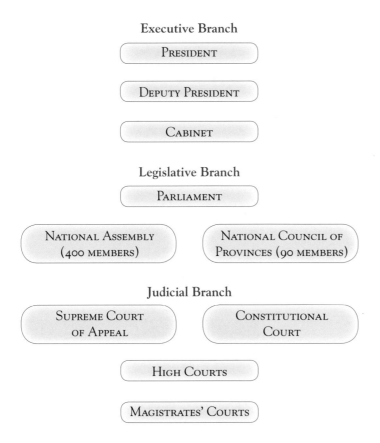

NATIONAL GOVERNMENT OF SOUTH AFRICA

Executive Branch

PRESIDENT

DEPUTY PRESIDENT

CABINET

Legislative Branch

PARLIAMENT

NATIONAL ASSEMBLY (400 MEMBERS)

NATIONAL COUNCIL OF PROVINCES (90 MEMBERS)

Judicial Branch

SUPREME COURT OF APPEAL

CONSTITUTIONAL COURT

HIGH COURTS

MAGISTRATES' COURTS

net made up of a deputy president and ministers. Each minister is in charge of a different policy area, such as education, energy, and health. The president appoints the members of the cabinet.

South Africa's parliament is based in Cape Town and has two houses, the National Assembly and the National Council of Provinces. The National Assembly has four hundred members who are elected to five-year terms. The National Council of Provinces has ninety members. Each of the nation's nine provincial legislatures elects ten of the members.

South Africa's Capitals

South Africa is unique in that it has three capital cities. One is the legislative capital, one is the administrative capital, and one is the judicial capital.

Cape Town, the legislative capital, is home to Parliament. Situated on the southwest coast of the nation, Cape Town's architecture reveals its early Dutch history. The city enjoys a pleasant climate most of the year, although the winter winds blowing off the Atlantic Ocean sometimes force people to cling to lampposts as they walk. The city is a major seaport welcoming both cruise ships and cargo ships. The city's skyline is dominated by Table Mountain. The city is renowned for its beautiful beaches and dramatic drives.

Pretoria (Tshwane), the administrative capital, is located in the northeast of South Africa. Government sessions are held in the Union Building, which sits on a hilltop overlooking the city. Pretoria was once considered an Afrikaner city. Today, Pretoria is a multilingual and multicultural city. One of the city's most notable sites is the Voortrekker Monument, which lies on the

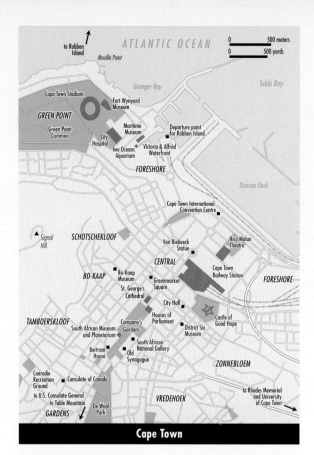

Cape Town

outskirts of the city. This massive stone building commemorates the triumph of the Afrikaners over the Zulus at the Battle of Blood River in 1838. On a hill facing the monument, the government has built Freedom Park, which honors the people who fought for freedom and equality in South Africa.

Bloemfontein (left), also called Mangaung, is the nation's judicial capital. It is the site of the Supreme Court of Appeal, the highest court in the country. The city, which is in central South Africa, has a pleasant climate, and the name Bloemfontein means "fountain of flowers." This is a good description of the city, because it is filled with flowers and hosts an annual rose festival. One of the city's greatest claims to fame is that it is the birthplace of J. R. R. Tolkien, the author of *The Hobbit* and the Lord of the Rings series.

The Judicial System

South Africa's highest court for constitutional issues is the Constitutional Court. It deals with such matters as whether new laws follow the constitution. The Supreme Court of Appeal is the highest regular court in South Africa. It hears appeals from lower courts. The president appoints the judges on both of these courts. Minor crimes are tried in magistrates' courts. More serious crimes are tried in high courts.

Provincial and Traditional Governments

South Africa has nine provinces. Each province has a premier who oversees a legislature that passes laws for that province. These laws must not conflict with national laws. The elected members of the provincial legislatures choose the premiers.

The Union Buildings in Pretoria house the president's offices.

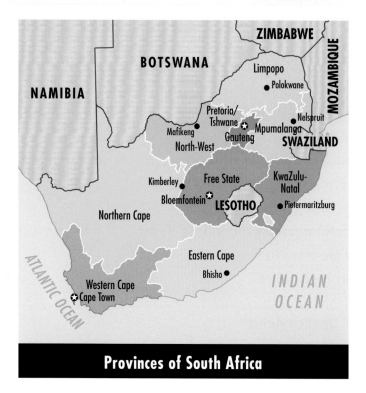

Provinces of South Africa

In keeping with its traditional heritage, South Africa also recognizes the authority of traditional leaders. These are men and women who are chiefs of their communities. In the past, they were the only figures of authority. They upheld the laws of their people, decided punishment for crimes, allocated land, and made treaties with other chiefs. Their authority was based on customary law, the law of the ethnic group. The new South African constitution recognizes their roles and allows them to act on matters that affect their own community.

South Africa's Flag

South's Africa national flag, which was adopted in 1994, was designed to represent all the different groups in the country and unite them under one symbol. The flag combines red, black, white, green, blue, and yellow in a geometric design. Bands of red and blue run across the top and the bottom, and a green Y shape runs horizontally through the middle. On the left is a black triangle framed in yellow. The six colors represent the nation's racial groups and reflect the country's past, present, and future. The flag that it replaced included small versions of the British flag and two former Boer republics. It did not represent black Africans, the majority of the citizens, at all.

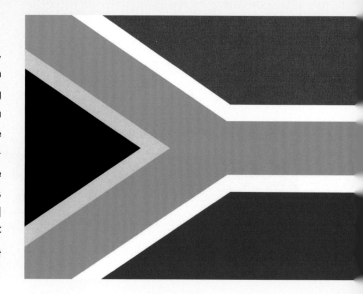

The National Anthem

In 1897, a Xhosa teacher named Enoch Sontonga wrote a song called "Nkosi Sikelel' iAfrika," ("Lord Bless Africa"). It became the anthem of the African National Congress. In 1994, when all South Africans were free to choose their president in the first national elections open to all races, "Nkosi Sikelel' iAfrika" became the country's national anthem. For a time, both this song and the former anthem, "Die Stem van Suid-Afrika" ("The Call of South Africa") were official anthems. Today, the official anthem is a combination of these two songs. The new anthem is unusual in that it is multilingual, including lyrics in five different languages.

Language	Lyrics	English translation
isiXhosa	Nkosi sikelel' iAfrika	Lord bless Africa
	Maluphakanyisw' uphondo lwayo,	Raise high her glory.
isiZulu	Yizwa imithandazo yethu,	Hear our prayers,
	Nkosi sikelela,	Lord bless us,
	thina lusapho lwayo.	We are her children.
Sesotho	Morena boloka setjhaba sa heso,	God protect our nation,
	O fedise dintwa la matshwenyeho,	End all wars and tribulations
	O se boloke, O se boloke setjhaba sa heso,	Protect us, protect our nation,
	Setjhaba sa South Afrika—South Afrika.	Our nation South Africa—South Africa.
Afrikaans	Uit die blou van onse hemel,	From the blue of our heaven,
	Uit die diepte van ons see,	From the depths of our sea,
	Oor ons ewige gebergtes,	Over our eternal mountain ranges,
	Waar die kranse antwoord gee,	Where the cliffs give answer,
English	Sounds the call to come together,	
	And united we shall stand,	
	Let us live and strive for freedom,	
	In South Africa our land.	

Powering a
Continent

S OUTH AFRICA'S WEALTH CAN BE COUNTED IN minerals, natural beauty, and the many cultures that make up the nation. These three elements come together to create a unique economy. South Africa stands out among the fifty-four nations on the African continent. It accounts for about one-quarter of all the goods and services produced on the continent. Its economy is very diversified. That means it does not count on any one industry or mineral for its wealth. It has major industries, abundant natural resources, an educated workforce, and a modern system of roads. Together, these elements have helped create a powerful economy.

Opposite: **Table Mountain rises above the harbor at the Victoria and Alfred Waterfront, a popular shopping area in Cape Town.**

Agriculture

Much of the land in South Africa is quite dry, so only about 13.5 percent of the land is suitable for farming. Corn is the nation's leading crop. Other important crops include wheat, sugarcane, peanuts, grapefruit, and pears. Grapes are grown at hundreds of vineyards, which produce world-class wine. South Africa also has a major dairy industry. South Africans also raise sheep, cattle, goats, and pigs for meat.

Fishing is a major industry in South Africa. The richest fishing areas lie off the western and southern coasts. Important catches includes pilchard, sole, and hake.

Manufacturing

About thirty-six thousand people work in South Africa's automobile industry.

Manufacturing accounts for about 15 percent of South Africa's economy. Food and beverage processing are among the most important manufacturing industries. This includes refining sugar and canning fish, fruit, and other products.

South Africa also has a large automobile industry. About a half million cars are produced in the country every year. Textile manufacturing is important in South Africa, as is the production of iron, steel, and chemicals.

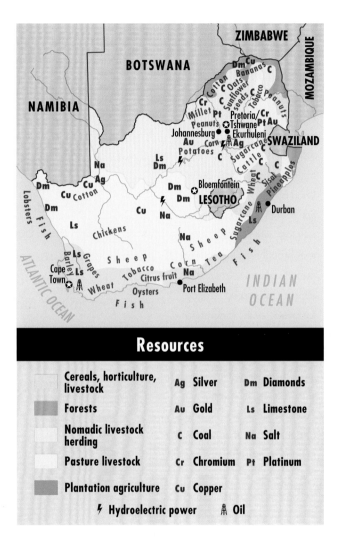

Mining

South Africa is rich in precious metals and stones. South Africa's gold mines are among the oldest in the world and have been producing steadily since gold was discovered there in 1886. South Africa's enormous gold reserves are concentrated in a small area, the Witwatersrand, near Johannesburg.

Gold production was the economic engine of South Africa for a long time. Over the last forty years, production has decreased by 80 percent. But South Africa's gold production is still ranked fifth in the world. In 2011, the country produced 221 metric tons of gold. The price of gold is set by world markets, so an ounce of gold mined anywhere in the world sells for exactly the same price. In 2012, gold producers were encouraged to mine as much as possible, because that year the price of gold was high—averaging more than US$1,600 per ounce.

South Africa also produces about three-quarters of the world's platinum. Platinum is used in making many products, including jewelry and engine parts for automobiles.

South Africa was the world's major producer of diamonds for many years. Some of South Africa's diamond mines are old and deep. The deeper a mine goes, the more expensive it is to bring out the precious material.

Although older mines are less profitable to work than they were in the past because their resources are fewer, they still have precious reserves. De Beers Consolidated Mines dominated the diamond industry for many years. Now, with its most important mines more than a century old, De Beers believed they were not profitable enough and sold them. Some historic diamond mines, including Kimberley, are now being worked by

Workers bring up rock from deep within a gold mine.

Bringing Up the Gold

Gold has been both a blessing and a curse for South Africa. While the economic advantage is obvious, the need for many workers to do the difficult, dirty, and dangerous job of mining underground has created a unique class of laborers. The miners work deep within the earth. There they clear away rocks, drill holes, and help load the ore onto conveyor belts.

The older the mine the deeper the mine is, and few mines are deeper than those in South Africa. Some of the mines go as deep as 2 miles (3 km). The miners have to take elevators far into the earth to reach the work site. It takes so long to go down, the miners spend their entire shifts underground. The mines are also located far away from the traditional living areas of many of the miners. Because of this, they are separated from their families while working at the mines.

The gold is found in tiny grains stuck within rock. It has to be blasted free. It is then treated with toxic chemicals to release it from the rock. This process is hard on the people doing the work and hard on the environment.

smaller companies. By keeping the mines operating, these companies provide employment for longtime miners. Hard work is better than no work at all.

De Beers has also found new sources of diamonds within South Africa. In 1992, the company opened the Venetia Diamond Mine in Limpopo Province in the north of the country. It was the first new diamond mine to open in many years. Many people thought it would be the last, but in 2008, the Voorspoed mine was opened. Located in the Free State Province in the central part of the country, it is a modern mine that meets high standards in environmental practices. The mine is unusual in other ways as well.

A worker in Kimberley examines a diamond.

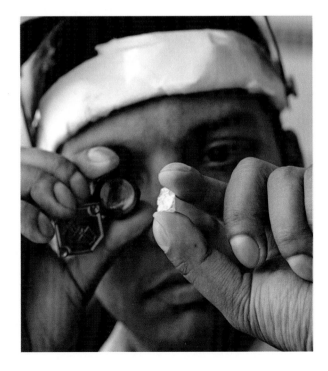

What South Africa Grows, Makes, and Mines

Agriculture (2009)

Sugarcane	20,500,000 metric tons
Corn	12,050,000 metric tons
Wheat	1,959,000 metric tons

Manufacturing (2010, value in sales)

Food products	US$28,462,000,000
Transportation equipment	US$18,513,000,000
Chemicals	US$14,883,000,000

Mining (2010, value in sales)

Platinum	US$8,450,000,000
Coal	US$7,950,000,000
Gold	US$6,080,000,000

For example, women hold at least 25 percent of the technical and mining jobs. In the older mines, all of the employees were men.

Services

Services make up the largest part of the South African economy. Service industries include education, health, sales, and banking. Many people in South Africa work in finance and trade.

Tourism is a booming service industry in South Africa. Eight million foreign tourists traveled to South Africa in 2010. People visit South Africa for many reasons. They come for the wildlife, the oceans, and the mountains. South Africa is an excellent place to eat fine food and drink excellent wines. Many tourists come to see the work of local artists and craftspeople. Some tourists travel the "crafts route," which includes visits to small shops and galleries where craftspeople can be viewed at work. Many South African craftspeople started their businesses by using discarded materials. This kind of recycling was necessary for people who couldn't afford to buy new materials.

South Africa also has a thriving fashion industry. Fashion photographers have been flocking to South Africa for years. When it is winter in Europe and the United States, it is summer in South Africa and a perfect time to have photo shoots outdoors.

The Chance to Shop

During apartheid, modern shopping malls filled the wealthy areas of South African suburbs. But many people in South Africa had little or no access to shops. For example, at that time, at least one million blacks lived in Soweto. The white government claimed that they lived there only on a temporary basis and were officially residents of one of ten homelands. As a result, there were no supermarkets in Soweto. Instead, there were only small corner shops. Soweto residents had to do their shopping in Johannesburg, where they were allowed to work. By not allowing permanent shops in Soweto and other black townships, the government kept complete control of the economy in those areas.

In 2007, after a long, long wait, a huge shopping mall opened in Soweto. The Maponya Mall has two hundred stores and an eight-screen movie theater. It also houses a statue of Hector Pieterson, a teenager who was killed in Soweto in 1976, during antiapartheid protests. Nelson Mandela attended the opening of the mall. His appearance signified the importance of this shopping mall to all the residents.

Money Facts

South Africa's currency is called the rand. It is an Afrikaans word that comes from the Witwatersrand, the ridge of land where South Africa's vast gold reserves were found. Each rand is divided into one hundred cents. In 2012, 1 rand equaled US$0.12, and US$1.00 equaled 8.34 rand.

Coins come in values of 1, 2, and 5 rand and 10 and 20 cents. The size of the coin increases with the value. Bills come in values of 10, 20, 50, 100, and 200 rand. In 2012, South Africa introduced a new design for its bills. Each banknote now includes an image of former president Nelson Mandela. The backs of the bills depict five of the largest mammals in South Africa. The 10-rand note shows a rhinoceros, while the 20-round note features elephants, and the 50-rand bill shows a lion. The 100-rand note depicts a fierce Cape buffalo, and the 200-rand note shows a beautiful leopard.

South Africa has also become a favorite location for filmmakers, who rely on its excellent weather, diverse backdrops,

Informal outdoor markets such as this one selling crafts are common in South Africa.

A model poses in a Cape Town fashion show. Cape Town has become a center of the fashion world.

and low costs. The film industry in South Africa first began to take off when people started making commercials there, taking advantage of the beautiful landscapes. Now, South Africa is promoting itself to the worldwide film community. In 2012, a team from South Africa traveled to France for the Cannes International Film Festival, the world's most prestigious film festival, to introduce their country's attractions and modern facilities to the world's film producers.

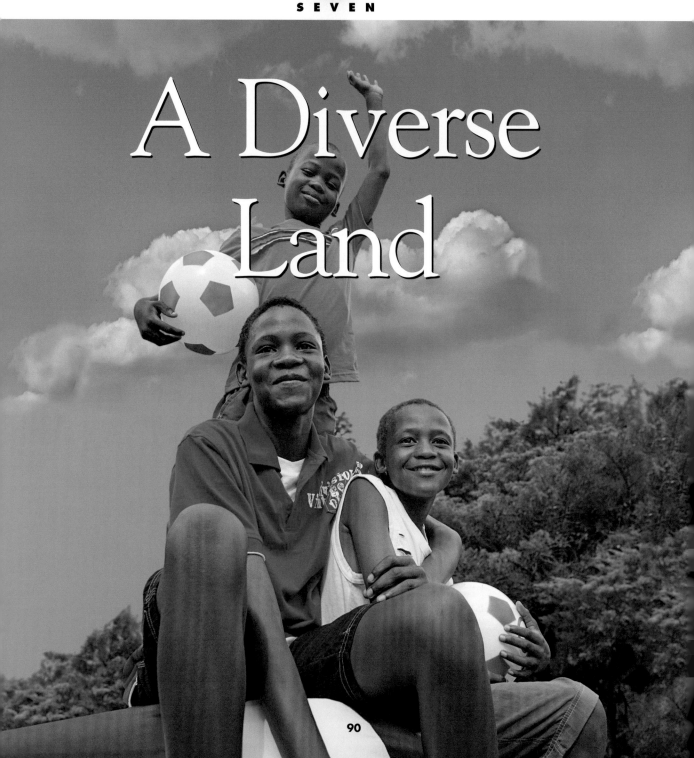

A Diverse Land

Opposite: **More than 28 percent of South Africans are under age fifteen.**

Language is at the heart of culture. The changes in attitude toward the use of language, and the teaching of language, show how much South Africa has changed since the end of apartheid. In 1976, black South Africans rose up in protest against the forced use of Afrikaans, the language of the white minority government. Black South African high school students wanted to be instructed in English, a language used in many countries in Africa and around the world. Afrikaans was used only in South Africa.

Many Languages

When apartheid ended, South Africa wrote a new constitution. One of its most cherished provisions was a new language policy. This policy recognized that South Africa's fifty million people make up a diverse, multiracial, multicultural population. While most countries have one or two official languages, South Africa has eleven: Afrikaans, English, Sepedi, Sesotho,

Who Lives in South Africa?

Black African	79.5%
White	9.0%
Coloured	9.0%
Indian/Asian	2.5%

Setswana, siSwati, Tshivenda, Xitsonga, isiNdebele, isiXhosa, and isiZulu. Many people speak more than one language.

The constitution recognizes that other languages are also used in South Africa. The constitution protects these languages. It instructs local officials to help speakers of these languages in their dealings with the government.

In the townships, many people can speak four languages. As children, people learn the language of their ethnic group. A second language may be acquired through marriage to someone from another ethnic group. Most people who work in South Africa's cities also learn English and Afrikaans. News programs use English as well as one of the other official languages.

The most widely spoken language among black South Africans is isiZulu, followed closely by isiXhosa. Among white South Africans, Afrikaans is spoken by about 60 percent of the people, and English is spoken by 40 percent. Many Afrikaners can speak English. Afrikaans is the first language of about 80 percent of the mixed-race population. The rest speak English as their first language.

Common isiZulu Phrases

Sawubona	Hello
Yebo	Yes
Cha	No
Kunjani?	How are you?
Ngiyabonga	Thank you
Mana kancane	One minute!

Mining Language

People who work in South Africa's mines speak many different languages. To allow them to communicate easily, a new group of words was invented for use in the mines. This is called Fanagalo, and it means "like this." It is based on isiZulu, which is widely used and understood.

Endangered Cultures

Of all the ethnic groups that live in South Africa, it is the San people, or Bushmen people, whose way of life has nearly disappeared. It is believed that there are about ten thousand San in South Africa. Their culture is still alive at !Khwa ttu, an educa-

In South Africa, signs often appear in a number of languages.

tion center near the town of Darling in the Western Cape. The San once had great knowledge of the plants in their homeland and how to use them as medicine. At this center, young San are once again learning about traditional medicines and the skills that kept their people alive for nearly thirty thousand years.

A San man paints an ostrich egg. Traditionally, the San used ostrich eggs as water containers.

The Malay people are the descendants of enslaved people who were brought to South Africa more than three hundred years ago. The Dutch brought them to South Africa from Southeast Asia. For generations, the Malay people were a tight-knit community that lived close to the center of Cape Town. Many of them were forced from their homes on the slopes of Table Mountain during the apartheid era, but a small group clung to their homes in a neighborhood called Bo-Kaap. Their charming houses are painted in bright colors and have become a symbol of Cape Town. In the past, these colors identified the type of worker who lived in the home: for example, tailor, carpenter, shoemaker, or builder. Today, rising property taxes are forcing many of the Malays out of Bo-Kaap.

Many Muslims of Indonesian and Malaysian descent live in the Bo-Kaap neighborhood of Cape Town.

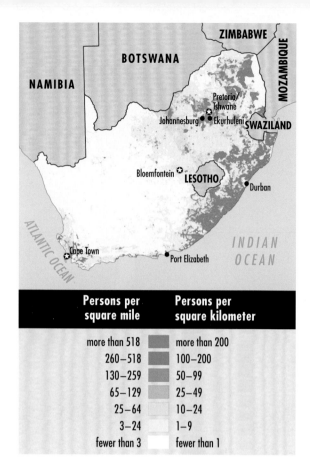

Persons per square mile	Persons per square kilometer
more than 518	more than 200
260–518	100–200
130–259	50–99
65–129	25–49
25–64	10–24
3–24	1–9
fewer than 3	fewer than 1

Cape Town is the only large city in western South Africa.

Population of major cities (2012 est.)

Johannesburg	3,607,000
Cape Town	3,353,000
Ekurhuleni (East Rand)	3,144,000
Durban	2,837,000
Pretoria	1,404,000

City and Country

Most people in South Africa live along the southern coast or in the eastern part of the country. Few people live in the west, except around Cape Town. The population density varies dramatically across the nine provinces. Gauteng, the smallest province, is home to Johannesburg, the financial center of the country. Nearly one-fourth of the total national population of some fifty million people lives in this province.

More than 60 percent of South Africans live in urban areas. Many of these are modern cities, but some are

In rural South Africa, some people live in traditional houses with straw roofs.

shantytowns that lack electricity and running water. The percentage of people in South Africa who live in urban areas is growing. More and more people are leaving the countryside in search of jobs in the city.

South Africa appears different to various groups of people. To visitors it has the look of any modern country. To the rising black middle class it is a land of promise, since the dream of a nonracial society has come true. To the millions who are still struggling, however, it feels like a very poor country.

Spiritual Ways

S OUTH AFRICA AS A NATION IS DEEPLY RELIGIOUS, but its many different people practice many different religions. Some are formal religions, with rituals that are recognized around the world. Others are traditional beliefs, practiced for hundreds of years, and specific to an ethnic group. Some people follow both a traditional religion and a formal religion, mixing the two and choosing the parts that best suit their lives. There is no official religion in South Africa.

Opposite: **Former archbishop Desmond Tutu baptizes a baby at the cathedral in Cape Town in 2008.**

Christianity and Apartheid

Christianity arrived in South Africa with the Dutch in the seventeenth century. These Christians worshipped in the Dutch Reformed Church.

The Dutch Reformed Church became the religion of the Afrikaner people. They interpreted the Bible very strictly. This included regarding people who were not white as inferior. This reading of the Bible became a reason to separate people of different races. In time, the Dutch Reformed Church became so closely connected with apartheid that some members of the church

Archbishop Desmond Tutu

Throughout his life and his career as leader of the Anglican Church of Southern Africa, Desmond Tutu fought against apartheid. He trained as a teacher, but he resigned his position after the government passed the Bantu Education Act, which restricted blacks to an inferior form of education. As a Christian and as a black African, he could not understand how other Christians considered black Africans and people of

mixed race to be less worthy than whites. He was criticized for expressing his views. He was also injured when he joined in marches and protests against apartheid. Despite this, he never lost his belief that racial equality would someday become the law of the land. In 1984, Tutu was awarded a Nobel Peace Prize for his lifelong efforts to bring peace and equality to all South Africans. In 1986, the Anglican Church named him Archbishop of South Africa, a position he held for ten years.

After apartheid ended, Archbishop Tutu headed the Truth and Reconciliation Commission. He has continued to use his strong moral authority to try to influence government officials to be humane and fair to all South Africans. He condemned them for failing to improve conditions for black South Africans.

considered it a sin to fight against it. Those who tried to fight apartheid from within the church paid heavily for their efforts.

Beyers Naudé, a Dutch Reformed minister was one of the most outspoken Afrikaners to protest against apartheid. The white South African government "banned" him for seven years. Banning meant he lived under house arrest and was not allowed to be in a room with more than one other person. In 1963, Beyers Naudé broke away from the Dutch Reformed Church and formed the Christian Institute. Eventually, the Dutch Reformed Church publicly apologized to black South Africans for its support of apartheid.

A Dutch Reformed building in the city of George on the southern coast.

Each year at Easter, more than a million members of the Zion Christian Church make a pilgrimage to the church's headquarters at Zion City at Moria. It is the largest Christian gathering in South Africa.

Christianity Today

Nearly 80 percent of all South Africans are Christian. The percentage is about the same for whites, blacks, and mixed-race people. About one-quarter of South African's Indians, descendants of those brought to work in the sugar plantations, are also Christians. The vast majority of South African Christians are Protestant. An estimated 7 to 8 percent of white churchgoers are Catholic.

Among black South Africans, the Zion Christian faith is the largest and fastest growing church. Engenas Lekganyane founded this church in South Africa in 1910. The Zion Christian Church offers a combination of Protestant beliefs and traditional African practices. It permits polygamy, meaning people can have more than one spouse at a time. It does not permit smoking, drinking alcohol, or eating pork. The highlight of the church's year is the Easter celebration. More than one million people gather for religious services at Zion City at Moria in the Northern Province.

Millions of South Africans follow other Protestant churches, including Methodist, Anglican, Lutheran, and Presbyterian. The Dutch Reformed Church is the largest Protestant church among whites and people of mixed race.

Catholics pray at the Cathedral of Christ the King in Johannesburg.

Christian	80%
Muslim	2.0%
Hindu	1.2%
Jewish	0.2%
Other beliefs	20%

*Total equals more than 100 percent because some people follow more than one belief.

Muslims attend a service at a mosque in Durban.

It is a strict form of Christianity. Some Dutch Reformed churches do not permit singing. The church buildings are very plain, without elaborate statues or decoration.

Other Faiths

Early Dutch settlers brought enslaved people from Indonesia and Malaysia in Southeast Asia to South Africa. These enslaved people brought the religion of Islam with them. In 1798, a mosque—a Muslim house of worship—was built in the Bo-Kaap section of Cape Town. It is the oldest mosque in South Africa. Today, about 2 percent of South Africans are Muslim.

In the 1860s, Indians were brought from India to Natal, an area of South Africa along the Indian Ocean, to work on sugarcane plantations. The Indians brought their own religions with them. Some of these people are Muslim; others are Hindu. Today, about 1 percent of South Africans are Hindu. Durban is the center of the Asian community in South Africa and is the site of many Hindu temples and Muslim mosques.

A small number of South Africans follow Judaism. The first Jewish synagogue in South Africa was built in Cape Town in 1863. Most South African Jews are descended from Lithuanians who fled religious persecution in Europe in the late 1800s. Today, South Africa is home to about seventy-five thousand Jews. Most of them live in the suburbs of Johannesburg and Cape Town.

South African dancers in Johannesburg join in a celebration of Diwali, an important Hindu festival. Diwali is sometimes known as the festival of lights because people display lit lanterns and candles to celebrate the triumph of good over evil.

Jews were at the forefront of the antiapartheid movement. Their most prominent voice was Helen Suzman, who died in 2009. She was a member of the liberal Progressive Party and served as the only antiapartheid voice in Parliament from 1961 to 1974. In spite of being harassed by the police, she was outspoken in her criticism of the National Party's apartheid policy. She served in Parliament for thirty-six years and lived to see the end of apartheid. In 2011, Western Boulevard in Cape Town was renamed Helen Suzman Boulevard in her honor.

Traditional Beliefs

Strong religious beliefs can take many forms. For many people, it is not necessary to go to a particular church building or follow a particular organized religion in order to express faith.

Many South Africans believe their ancestors play a large role in daily life. They believe that the spirits of all the people who came before them—their parents, aunts, uncles, grandparents—guide them from day to day and play a part in their decisions. South Africans believe they must honor and remember their ancestors' examples.

Traditional healers, or *sangomas*, are significant figures in many traditional faiths. Sangomas study their profession, learning how to use herbs and tree roots as natural medicines. They treat both physical and mental illnesses. Many sangomas are women. Some wear distinctive headdresses with strings of beads that cover their faces.

As a sangoma works with a patient, she looks at all the elements of that person's life. Because sangomas live in the same community as their patients, they usually know a great deal about them. This knowledge often gives them great skill in diagnosing a person's illness.

In 2007, the South African government recognized sangomas as legitimate healers under the Traditional Health Practitioners Act. It is estimated that about two hundred thousand traditional healers practice in South Africa. The plants they use have been studied by major drug companies. Many modern medicines have their origin in natural plants.

Sangomas use plant and animal products to treat illness. Many South Africans consult both sangomas and Western-style medical doctors.

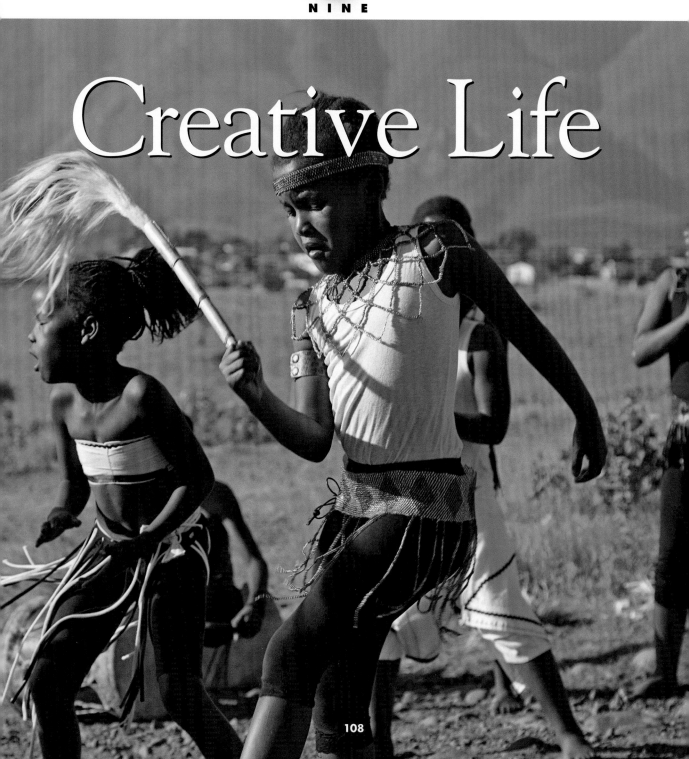

Creative Life

M ANY SOUTH AFRICANS HAVE MADE THEIR MARKS around the world in sports or arts. They have inspired their fellow South Africans through their brilliant words, music, and athletic achievements.

Opposite: **Dance is an important part of South African culture. Here, Xhosa children dance near their homes in the Western Cape province.**

Sports

Rugby and cricket are among the most popular sports in South Africa. The nation won the Rugby World Cup in 2007.

Football, known in the United States as soccer, is also hugely popular. In 2010, South Africa hosted the World Cup, the most-watched sporting event in the world. This month-long competition attracted teams and fans from all over the world. It was a chance for South Africa to show that it could stage a world-class sporting event. The tournament was successful and memorable. The *vuvuzelas*, noisy horns that fans blew throughout the matches, left a lasting impression. The vuvuzela is a traditional instrument made from the horn of the kudu, a large antelope. Modern vuvuzelas are made of plastic.

In July 2012, athletes from all over South Africa traveled to London, England, to take part in the Summer Olympics. They competed in many different events including boxing, cycling, equestrian, swimming, and track and field.

A boy blows on a vuvuzela during the 2010 World Cup tournament. Vuvuzelas are so loud that some sports leagues and stadiums have banned them.

South African swimmer Chad le Clos beat American Michael Phelps by five one-hundredths of a second to win the gold medal in the 200-meter butterfly at the 2012 Olympics.

For many years, South Africans were unable to take part in the Olympics. Beginning in 1964, the country's athletes were banned from Olympic competitions because of the apartheid system. In 1992, after the ban was lifted, runner Elana Meyer was the first athlete to compete for South Africa at the Olympics. She felt the weight of the entire nation on her shoulders.

In 2012, that weight was as light as a feather as the South African athletes brought home six Olympic medals: three golds, two silvers, and one bronze. Swimmers did particularly well. Cameron van der Burgh won gold in the men's 100-

Sprinter Oscar Pistorius was born without fibulas, major bones in the lower legs. Although his legs were amputated when he was a baby, he became a world-class athlete.

meter breaststroke, while Chad le Clos won gold in the men's 200-meter butterfly, beating American superstar swimmer Michael Phelps. Le Clos also won silver in the men's 100-meter butterfly. South Africa's third gold medal went to the four-man rowing team in the lightweight category. South African women were also successful. Caster Semenya won the silver medal in the women's 800-meter track race, and Bridgitte Hartley took a bronze in the women's 1,500-meter canoe race.

Oscar Pistorius, known as the Blade Runner, also competed at the Olympic Games. Pistorius's lower legs were amputated when he was young, and he runs wearing prostheses of curved metal blades. He took part in the men's 400-meter relay race, a first for a double-leg amputee in the Olympic Games. While the South African team did not win that race, Pistorius took home a gold medal in the 400-meter race at the Paralympics for disabled athletes in London in September 2012. South Africans won a total of twenty-nine medals at the Paralympic Games in 2012.

Go Fly a Kite

South Africans interested in taking part in their own sporting event can join in the annual Cape Town International Kite Festival in Muizenberg, a little town on False Bay on the southwest coast. As Africa's biggest kite festival, it attracts more than twenty thousand visitors, including kite makers from around the world.

Literature

Many great writers have made their mark in South Africa. Two South African writers have been awarded the Nobel Prize in Literature, the highest possible honor for a writer. Nadine Gordimer won in 1991 and J. M. Coetzee won in 2003. Many of Gordimer's novels, including *July's People* and *Burger's*

Novelist J. M. Coetzee has won many of the world's leading literary awards. He was the first person to win the Booker Prize, Britain's top literary prize, two times.

Daughter, deal with life under apartheid. Coetzee's works also explore the apartheid system. They include *In the Heart of the Country* and *Disgrace*.

Novelist and playwright Zakes Mda was born in 1948. His novel *The Heart of Redness* is set partly among the Xhosa in the 1800s. The South African newspaper the *Sunday Times*, awarded the novel its fiction prize in 2001.

Zakes Mda has written more than twenty books, including novels, plays, and a memoir.

Fabulous Puppets

In recent years, thousands of theatergoers have thrilled to the sight of life-size horse puppets moving like real horses onstage in the play *War Horse*. These puppets are the handiwork of Handspring Puppet Company, which is based in Cape Town. This company of craftspeople was formed in 1981 and quickly became known for shows for adults. When *War Horse* opened on Broadway, theatergoers were awed by how lifelike the horses were. The puppet makers used mechanics that moved the horses' heads and tails so realistically that the puppets seemed to actually come to life. Handspring Puppet Company received a Special Tony Award for its work in creating the horse puppets for the show.

Playwright Athol Fugard's dramas, such as *Master Harold . . . and the Boys*, have been staged on Broadway. They depict the difficult and often dangerous lives of their black and white characters. The Fugard Theatre, named in his honor, opened in Cape Town in 2011. It is located in a historic building in District Six.

Charlize Theron

Actress Charlize Theron is known around the world for her brave and powerful performances. She won an Academy Award in 2004 for her role in *Monster* and starred in *Snow White and the Huntsman* in 2012. Theron grew up on a farm near Benoni, South Africa. Grateful for all that she has been able to accomplish, she created the Africa Outreach Project, aimed at teaching schoolchildren about health-related issues.

Ladysmith Black Mambazo performs with their choir head, Joseph Shabalala (front).

Dance and Song

There are as many different types of music and dance in South Africa as there are cultural groups.

Zulu choirs are known for their complicated harmonies that create rich sound without the help of any musical instruments. The best-known Zulu choir is Ladysmith Black Mambazo. This group has traveled the world performing their own songs and working with many other artists, including American songwriter and musician Paul Simon.

Zulu dancing is exciting to watch. The dancers pound their feet in unison while chanting. Some dances imitate how men hunt animals, while others show men preparing for battle. The Zulus were traditionally known as powerful fighters.

The Malay people of Cape Town are known for the Kaapse Klopse New Year's festival they hold each January. The Malay choirs spend months preparing their colorful costumes and painting their faces before they dance their way through the streets of Bo-Kaap and District Six. During the festival, troupes of performers march in unison while hundreds of thousands of onlookers line the streets to cheer them on. Today, people of all backgrounds take part in the festival.

Thousands of marchers join the parades during the Kaapse Klopse.

The Reed Dance

The Zulu reed dance had not been performed for many years when Zulu king Goodwill Zwelithini decided to bring it back in 1984. He believed that young people needed to become reacquainted with their own culture after many years of being influenced by Western ideas. This dance is performed by girls dressed in traditional beads. They carry reeds that have just been harvested. These reeds are brought to the royal residence. In the past, the reeds were used to rebuild the kraal, the fence that protected the queen mother's cattle. Now the reeds are mainly symbolic. The pride the dancers show, however, is traditional.

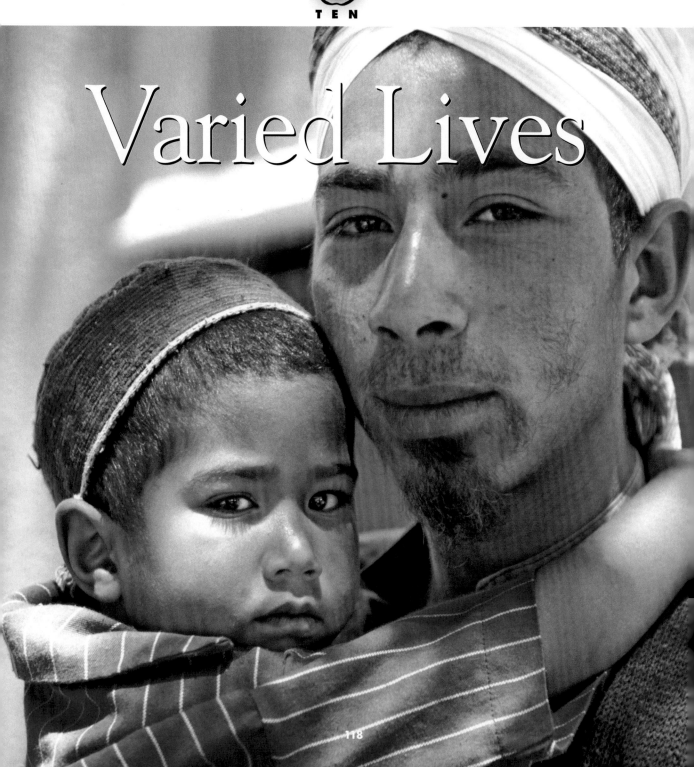

Varied Lives

A TYPICAL DAY FOR A PERSON LIVING IN SOUTH Africa depends entirely on where that person lives. For middle-class city folk, daily life is filled with going to work, taking care of the family and home, and enjoying weekends off. To relax, an urban South African might go to a museum or an art gallery, or take a drive along one of South Africa's beautiful scenic routes. Shopping for food means a trip to a modern supermarket with a wide variety of foods, including imported items.

For the millions of people who live in the townships, there is little time for leisure activities. Days are filled with getting the basic needs of life. For those who have jobs, travel to work can take more than an hour in crowded minivans, known locally as taxis. After work, women spend time preparing food for their families. They use very basic cooking equipment and often don't have refrigerators. The meals are simple, usually consisting of a porridge called mealie pap, made from cornmeal. The women might make a stew with meat and vegetables bought that same day.

Opposite: **A father and son in Cape Town. Family is central to South African life.**

Public Holidays

New Year's Day	January 1
Human Rights Day	March 21
Good Friday	March or April
Easter Monday	March or April
Freedom Day	April 27
Workers' Day	May 1
Youth Day	June 16
National Women's Day	August 9
Heritage Day (right)	September 24
Day of Reconciliation	December 16
Christmas Day	December 25
Day of Goodwill	December 26

But no matter where they live, South Africans devote much of their time to their families.

Good Eating

The different cultures in South Africa each have their own style of cooking. One popular dish is *bobotie*, a delicious type of spiced, minced meat. It has a distinctly South African flavor, thanks to the chutney and curry powder used in it. Bunny chow is a common street food in South Africa. It starts with a loaf of bread that is hollowed out. The bread is filled with either vegetarian or meat curry. Each cook's version is different. Bunny chow, which originated in the Indian community of Durban, is the number one take-out food in South Africa.

Boerewors is another South African favorite. Boerewors are sausages made from lamb, veal, pork, or other meats. The spices used to make Boerewors differ from family to family and from farm to farm. Boerewors are usually grilled outdoors during *braais*, the Afrikaans word for barbecue.

Boerewors are usually made in the form of a long spiral.

Bobotie

A few special ingredients spice up this meat loaf. Have an adult help you with this recipe.

Ingredients

2 tablespoons vegetable oil

2 medium onions, minced

1½ pounds ground beef

1 cup milk

2 thick slices of bread, toasted

½ cup raisins

1 teaspoon apricot jam

½ tablespoon curry powder

1 teaspoon salt

½ teaspoon ground black pepper

1 large egg

1 pinch salt

Directions

Preheat the oven to 350°F and lightly grease a 9 x 13 inch baking dish. Heat the oil in a large skillet over medium-high heat. Cook the onions in the hot oil until they are soft. Next, crumble the ground beef into the skillet and cook it until it is brown.

Pour the milk into a shallow dish and soak the bread in the milk. Squeeze the excess milk from the bread and set the milk aside. Add the bread to the beef mixture. Stir in the raisins, jam, curry powder, salt, and black pepper. Pour the mixture into the baking dish.

Bake for one hour. While the meat loaf is baking, combine the remaining milk, egg, and salt. Pour this mixture over the top of the dish and return it to the oven. Let it bake until the top is golden brown, about 25 to 30 minutes. Enjoy!

Housing

South African housing ranges from grand homes with gardens and the best modern conveniences to shacks made out of zinc metal sheets. People looking for work have built these shacks near major cities. They make a home of whatever materials they can find. Advertising posters are often used to line the walls inside, helping to keep out the cold and wind. There is little that can be done to keep out the rain.

Pretty houses line a road in Cape Town.

Getting Water

One of the major chores for women and girls is a daily trip to get water for use in the home. Millions of people do not have access to water in their homes. Many live in townships that were built as a temporary place to live. Even though these houses have been lived in by generations of people, not all have been upgraded. For people living in the townships, this usually means walking to a water faucet that serves a large number of houses. For people in rural areas, it can mean walking long distances carrying heavy pails of water on their heads.

One solution to the problem of getting water is a device called Imvubu, a Zulu word that means "hippo." The Imvubu is a large water can on rollers. It has made a huge difference in the rural areas where it has been introduced. Instead of children and women walking a mile to a stream to collect water many times a day, a person can push home 24 gallons (90 liters) at once.

Going to School

In South Africa, children are required to attend school from ages seven through sixteen, or through grade nine, whichever comes first. Students are taught in one of the nation's eleven official languages.

The South African constitution guarantees children the right to an education, but schools suffered serious neglect during the apartheid era. It will take many years and a lot of funds to improve the schools.

In the meantime, local solutions are being found for the enormous task of educating South Africa's millions of chil-

dren. The government has not been able to keep up with the demand for schools that teach the subjects children need in a modern society. Private schools, funded by many different groups and foundations, are stepping in to fill this need. One of the most successful is LEAP (for Langa Educational Assistance Program), which aims at educating children from the townships where there is little opportunity and a huge need for schooling. LEAP students spend a long day at school working on math, science, and English.

One of the best-known schools in South Africa is the Oprah Winfrey Leadership Academy for Girls in Henley-on-Klip, south of Johannesburg. Founded by the American TV

All public schools in South Africa require children to wear uniforms.

personality in 2007, the school offers girls from all races a chance at a good education. The first group of seventy-two students graduated in 2012. Every graduate has been accepted to college and offered a full scholarship.

The University of South Africa in Pretoria is the largest university in Africa. Other major universities include the University of Johannesburg, the University of Pretoria, and Nelson Mandela Metropolitan University in Port Elizabeth and George.

The University of Cape Town was founded in 1829. It is the oldest university in South Africa.

Young dancers perform at the National Arts Festival.

Expressing Their Culture

Each summer, hundreds of thousands of South Africans attend the National Arts Festival in Grahamstown, near the southern coast. This eleven-day festival showcases every form of artistic expression South Africa has to offer. It includes classical and contemporary theater, ballet, jazz, crafts, art exhibitions, comedy, opera, and even puppet shows performed in many languages by people of different ethnicities. At this festival, the entire nation of South Africa is on display in all its diversity.

Timeline

South African History		World History	
The San inhabit the region.	30,000 BCE		
The Bantu migrate into what is now South Africa.	300 CE		
		ca. 2500 BCE	The Egyptians build the pyramids and the Sphinx in Giza.
		ca. 563 BCE	The Buddha is born in India.
		313 CE	The Roman emperor Constantine legalizes Christianity.
		610	The Prophet Muhammad begins preaching a new religion called Islam.
		1054	The Eastern (Orthodox) and Western (Roman Catholic) Churches break apart.
		1095	The Crusades begin.
		1215	King John seals the Magna Carta.
		1300s	The Renaissance begins in Italy.
		1347	The plague sweeps through Europe.
		1453	Ottoman Turks capture Constantinople, conquering the Byzantine Empire.
		1492	Columbus arrives in North America.
Portuguese explorer Bartolomeu Dias becomes the first European to reach South Africa.	1488		
		1500s	Reformers break away from the Catholic Church, and Protestantism is born.
Jan van Riebeeck arrives from Holland and establishes Cape Town.	1652		
The Boers begin to trek inland, away from the Cape region.	1770s		
		1776	The U.S. Declaration of Independence is signed.
The British take over the Cape colony.	1795		
		1789	The French Revolution begins.

South African History

Shaka becomes king of the Zulus.	**1816**
British settlers arrive and form an English-speaking community.	**1820**
The Boers embark on the Great Trek.	**1834**
Boers and Zulus battle at Blood River.	**1838**
Diamonds are discovered near Orange River.	**1867**
Gold is discovered on the Witwatersrand.	**1886**
The Second Boer War begins.	**1899**
The British form the Union of South Africa.	**1910**
The Union of South Africa enacts the Natives Land Act, restricting where blacks can own land.	**1913**
The National Party wins the general election and begins enacting apartheid laws.	**1948**
The government bans the ANC and PAC; police kill dozens of black South Africans in the Sharpeville Massacre.	**1960**
Police kill thirteen-year-old Hector Pieterson during the Soweto uprising.	**1976**
F. W. de Klerk is elected president.	**1989**
Nelson Mandela is released from prison.	**1990**
Nelson Mandela is elected president.	**1994**
South Africa hosts the World Cup.	**2010**

World History

1865	The American Civil War ends.
1879	The first practical lightbulb is invented.
1914	World War I begins.
1917	The Bolshevik Revolution brings communism to Russia.
1929	A worldwide economic depression begins.
1939	World War II begins.
1945	World War II ends.
1969	Humans land on the Moon.
1975	The Vietnam War ends.
1989	The Berlin Wall is torn down as communism crumbles in Eastern Europe.
1991	The Soviet Union breaks into separate states.
2001	Terrorists attack the World Trade Center in New York City and the Pentagon near Washington, D.C.
2004	A tsunami in the Indian Ocean destroys coastlines in Africa, India, and Southeast Asia.
2008	The United States elects its first African American president.

Fast Facts

Official name: Republic of South Africa

Capitals: Pretoria (Administrative), Cape Town (Legislative), Bloemfontein (Judicial)

Official languages: Afrikaans, English, Sepedi, Sesotho, Setswana, siSwati, Tshivenda, Xitsonga, isiNdebele, isiXhosa, and isiZulu

Bloemfontein

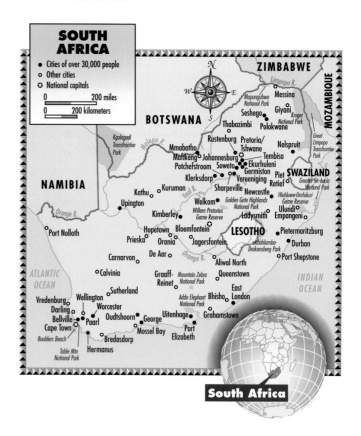

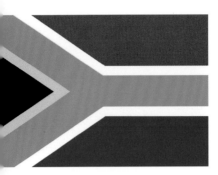

South African flag

Official religion:	None
National anthem:	"Nkosi Sikelel' iAfrika" ("Lord Bless Africa")
Type of government:	Republic
Head of state and government:	President
Area of country:	471,359 square miles (1,220,814 sq km)
Bordering countries:	Namibia to the northwest; Botswana to the north; Zimbabwe to the northeast; Mozambique and Swaziland to the east. Lesotho is in the center-east and is completely surrounded by South Africa.
Highest elevation:	Njesuthi, 11,181 feet (3,408 m)
Lowest elevation:	Sea level along the coast
Average high temperature:	In Johannesburg, 78°F (26°C) in January; 62°F (17°C) in July
Average low temperature:	In Johannesburg, 59°F (15°C) in January; 39°F (4°C) in July
Average annual rainfall:	28 inches (71 cm) in Johannesburg; 20 inches (51 cm) in Cape Town

Cape of Good Hope

Kruger National Park

National population (2012 est.): 48,810,427

Population of major cities (2012 est.):

Johannesburg	3,607,000
Cape Town	3,353,000
Ekurhuleni (East Rand)	3,144,000
Durban	2,837,000
Pretoria	1,404,000

Landmarks:

▶ *Cape Agulhas*, Cape Town

▶ *Kruger National Park*, near Nelspruit

▶ *Museum Africa*, Johannesburg

▶ *Nelson Mandela Statue*, Groot Drakenstein Prison, near Cape Town

▶ *Table Mountain*, Cape Town

Economy: South Africa has great mineral wealth. The country is the fourth-biggest gold producer in the world and also mines diamonds, platinum, and coal. It manufactures a broad variety of products including iron, steel, textiles, chemicals, and vehicles. Food and beverage processing are major industries. In agriculture, the country supplies corn, poultry, beef cattle, and many types of fruits and vegetables.

Currency

Currency: The South African rand. In 2012, 1 rand equaled US$0.12, and US$1.00 equaled 8.34 rand.

System of weights and measures: Metric system

Literacy rate (2006): 86.4%

Schoolchildren

Charlize Theron

Common isiZulu words and phrases:

Sawubona	Hello.
Yebo	Yes
Cha	No
Kunjani?	How are you?
Ngiyabonga	Thank you
Mana kancane	One minute!

Prominent South Africans:

Steve Biko (1946–1977)
Antiapartheid leader

Athol Fugard (1932–)
Playwright

Nadine Gordimer (1923–)
Winner of the Nobel Prize in Literature

Nelson Mandela (1918–)
President, antiapartheid leader

Zakes Mda (1948–)
Writer

Helen Suzman (1917–2009)
Member of Parliament

Charlize Theron (1975–)
Actor

Desmond Tutu (1931–)
Anglican archbishop and political activist

To Find Out More

Books

- Crompton, Samuel Willard. *Desmond Tutu: Fighting Apartheid.* New York: Chelsea House, 2008.

- Keller, Bill. *Tree Shaker: The Story of Nelson Mandela.* Boston: Kingfisher, 2008.

- Mace, Virginia. *South Africa.* Washington, D.C.: National Geographic, 2007.

Music

- Ladysmith Black Mambazo. *Ladysmith Black Mambazo: The Warner Bros. Collection.* Claremont, CA: Rhino Records, 2000.

- Putumayo Presents. *South Africa.* New York: Putumayo, 2010.

▶ Visit this Scholastic Web site for more information on South Africa:
www.factsfornow.scholastic.com
Enter the keywords **South Africa**

Index

Page numbers in *italics* indicate illustrations.

Meet the Authors

JASON LAURÉ AND ETTAGALE BLAUER HAVE BEEN following the story of South Africa since their first year-long journey through the country from 1977 to 1978. Over the years, they have observed the changing government, economy, and racial attitudes. They have talked with people all across the vast nation, driving on its fine roads and admiring the coastlines. They have gone deep into the gold and diamond mines and visited the vast Karoo. They have witnessed the initial moves toward ending apartheid in 1990 and were there in 1994 when South Africa held its first democratic election. They spent a year in South Africa researching their award-winning book *South Africa, Coming of Age Under Apartheid*. Lauré became so intrigued by South Africa and so optimistic about its future that he now makes his home in Cape Town.

Blauer made many long trips to South Africa over the past decades, gathering material for this new edition of *South Africa* in the Enchantment of the World series. She spent months in the country in the late 1990s working on her book *African Elegance*, which celebrates the crafts and cultures of sub-Saharan Africa.

Since the end of apartheid, the authors have seen dramatic changes in daily life in South Africa. They acknowledge the long road the country has to travel to bring economic freedom to the majority of its citizens. Both authors have high hopes for the nation's continued success.

Photo Credits